PRECIOUS JEWELLERY

Cheryl Owen

PRECIOUS JEWELLERY

NEW
HOLLAND

First published in 2009 by New Holland Publishers (UK) Ltd
London • Cape Town • Sydney • Auckland

Garfield House
86–88 Edgware Rd
London W2 2EA
United Kingdom

80 McKenzie Street
Cape Town 8001
South Africa

Unit 1
66 Gibbes Street
Chatswood
NSW 2067
Australia

218 Lake Road
Northcote
Auckland
New Zealand

ISBN 978 1 84773 357 3

Senior Editor Corinne Masciocchi
Designer Lucy Parissi
Photographer Paul Bricknell
Stylist Susie Johns
Production Laurence Poos
Editorial Direction Rosemary Wilkinson

1 3 5 7 9 10 8 6 4 2

Reproduction by PDQ Digital Media Solutions Ltd, UK
Printed and bound by Craft Print Pte Ltd, Singapore

CONTENTS

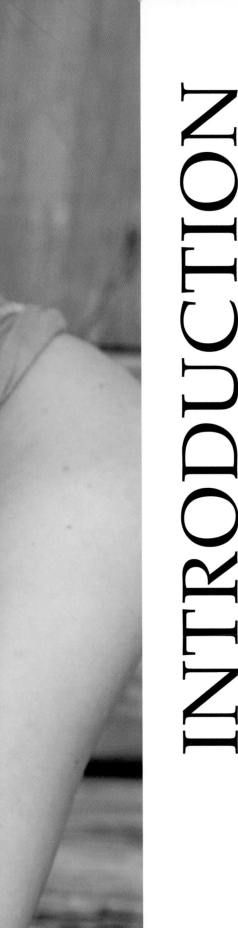

INTRODUCTION

It is great fun to create jewellery and also surprisingly easy. Only basic tools are required but the most exciting part is the fabulous choice of beads that is widely available nowadays. Once you start making jewellery with beautiful semi-precious, glass and crystal beads, you will not want to use anything else.

The projects in this book cater for all tastes and are accompanied by concise step-by-step instructions to help you achieve a professional standard. There are variations to each project that show the versatility of both the design and materials used. Most pieces are quick to make and once you have tackled a project, you can adapt the technique to make a matching necklace, bracelet or set of earrings.

Be inspired to use the techniques to create your own designs. Hand crafted jewellery makes wonderful gifts for friends and family – if you can bear to part with them!

EQUIPMENT

A surprisingly small amount of equipment is needed to make jewellery. For comfort and safety, work on a well lit, flat and clean surface. Keep sharp tools and materials beyond the reach of young children. Arrange beads on a non-slip surface so they do not run away when working out designs; a towel, piece of felt or fleece is ideal. Work on a white or skin-toned surface as a strong background will affect the appearance of the colours you use. Alternatively, use a bead board which has U-shaped grooves in which to arrange beads when designing a necklace.

TOOLS

(1) Tape measure and **ruler**: keep a tape measure and ruler handy. For a bracelet, measure the wrist with a tape measure but use a length of flexible beading wire to gauge the length of a necklace as a tape measure will not drape in the same way, then measure the beading wire with a tape measure or ruler.

(2) Wire snippers: use jewellery wire snippers to snip wire, including flexible beading wire.

(3) Snipe-nose pliers: these versatile pliers have flat-faced jaws to hold work in progress and to close calotte crimps and cord ends.

(4) Round-nose pliers: used to make neat loops.

(5) Crimping pliers: secure crimp beads with crimping pliers for a professional finish to your jewellery.

(6) Plastic-tipped pliers: the broad plastic jaws of these pliers should be used on delicate projects to prevent damaging the piece you are working on.

(7) Scissors: cut threads, cord and ribbon with embroidery scissors. Fine wire can be cut with an old pair of scissors but the metal will blunt the scissors.

(8) Needles: thread tiny beads and work bead weaving projects with beading needles, which come in short and long lengths and are very fine; size 10 is an all-round good size. Collapsible eye needles are flexible twisted wire needles, where the eye squeezes closed to pull through bead holes.

(9) Masking tape: use this low-tack adhesive tape to wrap around thread, bead cord and flexible beading wire to stop beads slipping off and to hold work temporarily in place.

(10) Mandrel: use a ring mandrel to form wire rings.

(11) Bead loom: weave a band of small beads on a bead loom to make a lariat, choker or bracelet.

(12) Bead reamer: enlarge the holes of glass and stone beads

with a diamond-tipped bead reamer. Apply gentle pressure when reaming to avoid chipping the bead.

(13) Adhesive: use cyanoacrylate adhesive or jeweller's cement to secure thread knots and to fill the

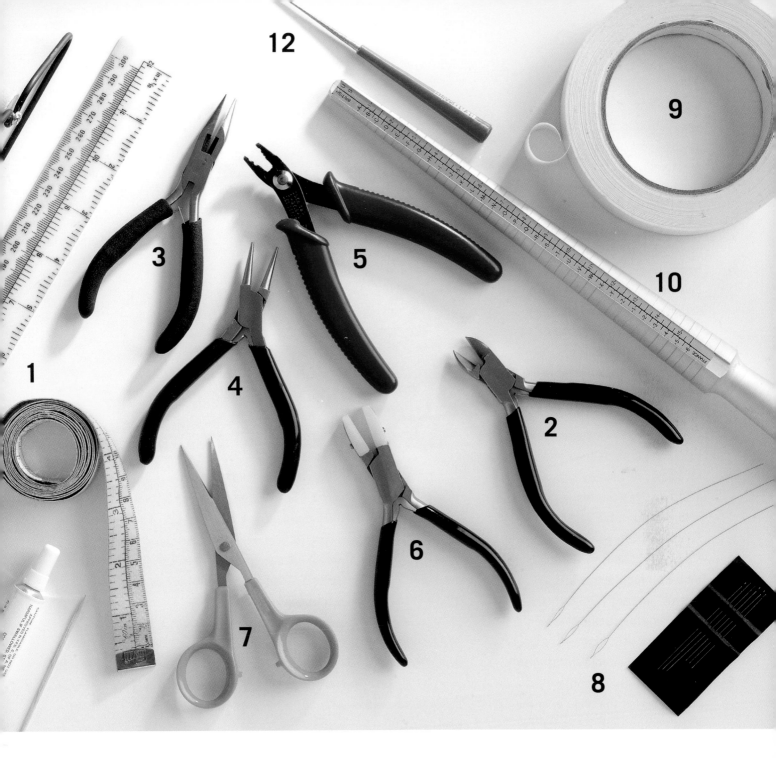

gap between the join of a jump ring or single loop. Apply a tiny dot of adhesive through a fine nozzle or apply the adhesive with the tip of a cocktail stick. Clear nail varnish can also be used on jewellery findings and to stiffen the ends of cotton cord and ribbon and to stop them fraying.

(14) Water or air erasable pen: although not essential, use a water- or air-erasable pen to mark threads and bead cords. This is useful to note the place to stop beading or to position a particular bead. Marks made with a water-erasable pen will disappear when wetted and marks made with an air-erasable pen will slowly fade away. The pens are available from haberdashery departments.

BEADS

The following pages showcase a selection of precious and semi-precious beads used throughout the book. Due to the popularity of beads, many small bead shops have sprung up recently and they are veritable treasure troves of goodies. The internet gives access to an endless selection of unusual beads and components without having to leave the comfort of your home. Also consider taking apart old broken jewellery to reuse the beads.

Beads get everywhere! Small beads such as delicas and rocailles are usually supplied in seal-top bags or plastic cylinders with plug-in lids. These containers are good for storing small items as they do not take up much space and are transparent for easy identification. Clear stubby containers with screw-on lids are widely available in different sizes. They are versatile containers as the wide opening allows you to slip a needle through the mass of beads to pick them up.

Tip large beads into shallow bowls or saucers when working. Keep beads in sealed containers at other times to protect them from dust, and store all beads away from direct sunlight.

METAL BEADS AND PEARLS

1. *Metallic coated delica beads* **2.** *3 mm (⅛ in) gold filled beads* **3.** *3 mm (⅛ in) sterling silver oval and 6 mm (¼ in) star shaped beads* **4.** *Galvanized silver delica beads* **5.** *2 cm (¾ in) sterling silver polos* **6.** *Mother-of-pearl carved crescent moons and butterflies* **7.** *Mother-of-pearl coins* **8.** *5 mm (¼ in) round mother-of-pearl beads and mother-of-pearl chips* **9.** *1.5 cm (⅝ in) dyed gold mother-of-pearl hexagon beads* **10.** *2 cm (¾ in) dyed magenta mother-of-pearl polos* **11.** *Gold long drilled freshwater pearls* **12.** *Rainbow long drilled freshwater pearls* **13.** *4 mm (⅙ in) pink potato freshwater pearls* **14.** *8 mm (⁵⁄₁₆ in) pale blue glass pearls* **15.** *7 mm (⁹⁄₃₂ in) white potato freshwater pearls* **16.** *6 mm (¼ in) cranberry potato and top drilled lilac button freshwater pearls* **17.** *7 mm (⁹⁄₃₂ in) fluro green freshwater pearls* **18.** *4 mm (⅙ in) turquoise baroque freshwater pearls* **19.** *4 mm (⅙ in) magenta potato freshwater pearls* **20.** *5 mm (¼ in) candy pink baroque freshwater pearls*

Metal beads and pearls

Metal beads: use sterling silver, gold-filled and vermeil beads as spacers between feature beads to stop the feature beads from overpowering a design. Delica beads are tiny cylindrical beads used for bead embroidery and weaving. Twenty-four karat gold, sterling silver and bronze-coated delicas are available. Bali silver beads are decorated with tiny silver balls and fine wires, giving the pieces an ethnic appeal.

Mother-of-pearl: mother-of-pearl is the iridescent nacre coating inside shells which can be carved into all sorts of shapes and dyes well. Mother-of-pearl and pearl jewellery are known as 'organic' jewellery because they are created from a living creature or plant.

Pearls: pearls are created in the shells of sea- and fresh-water molluscs and have been popular in jewellery-making since ancient Greek and Roman times. Cultured pearls are produced by pearl farmers and harvesters using a technique developed in Japan, a country that to this day provides most of the world's supply. Freshwater pearls are created in mussels and come mostly from China. Glass pearls have a lovely lustrous pearly coating and a crystal glass core which makes them reassuringly weighty.

Nowadays, pearls come in all sorts of shapes and sizes, and their names are a good indication of their shape. For instance, stick, coin, button and potato pearls are all available. White and natural shades are usually associated with pearls but lots of vibrant colours are also available.

Because pearls are delicate they can easily be scratched, and this is why there is a knot between each pearl in a traditional string of pearls so they do not rub together. Store pearls separately from other jewellery and avoid them coming into contact with perfume and cosmetics.

Glass beads and crystals

Hand-crafted glass beads are made using ancient techniques. They can incorporate metallic foils or crackles and have all sorts of surface decoration. Mass produced glass beads

GLASS BEADS AND CRYSTALS

1. *Iridescent glass rocaille beads* **2.** *Gold glass rocaille beads* **3.** *Millefiori beads* **4.** *1.2 cm (½ in) pink square foiled glass beads* **5.** *2 cm (¾ in) gold oval dichroic glass beads* **6.** *1 cm (⅜ in) lilac lamp beads* **7.** *5 mm (¼ in) pink pressed glass beads* **8.** *8 mm (⁵⁄₁₆ in) clear facetted square beads* **9.** *Blue drop lamp beads* **10.** *Assorted handmade glass beads* **11.** *6 mm (¼ in) tanzanite spacer crystal beads* **12.** *Facetted heart crystal beads* **13.** *Metal rondels studded with crystals* **14.** *8 mm (⁵⁄₁₆ in) crystal bicone crystal beads* **15.** *6 mm (¼ in) fuschia bicone and amethyst crystal beads* **16.** *8 mm (⁵⁄₁₆ in) siam bicone crystal beads* **17.** *4 mm (⅛ in) sapphire bicone crystal beads* **18.** *8 mm (⁵⁄₁₆ in) indicolite and 4 mm (⅛ in) jet AB bicone crystal beads* **19.** *4 mm (⁵⁄₃₂ in) mixed bicone crystal beads* **20.** *4 mm (⅛ in) amethyst AB2 and 6 mm (¼ in) violet opal bicone crystal beads*

are pressed or moulded into various shapes and sizes and come in many different finishes and colours.

Crystal is glass with more than 30 per cent lead content. It is the lead that gives crystal its high refractive quality, making it sparkle like a diamond. **Swarovski crystals** are the best quality. Crystal beads come in a wide colour range and in lots of facetted shapes; bicone crystals are particularly versatile. AB stands for Aurora Borealis and is the iridescent rainbow-like coating given to some crystals.

Rocaille beads are small inexpensive beads that are sold by weight and are used for bead weaving and embroidery. They are available in a huge colour range and lots of finishes.

Millefiori means 'thousand flowers'. These beautiful Venetian beads are created from thin glass rods which are bundled together then reheated and stretched so that the rods fuse together to make a flower-like pattern.

Lampwork beads are created by heating glass with a gas torch which is wound around a metal rod to form the base of the bead which can then be decorated with molten glass.

Dichroic glass beads have a thin layer of metal fused to the surface, which gives a metallic sheen that alters when viewed from different angles.

Semi-precious beads

A semi-precious stone is a natural stone mined from the earth that is not classed as a gem stone. Buying semi-precious chips is an inexpensive way of using a favourite stone.

Each month has a birth stone and many wedding anniversaries have designated stones. Bear this in mind and incorporate the relevant semi-precious beads if you are making jewellery as a gift. Many stones are believed to have healing qualities and would be a thoughtful feature of a well-wishing gift of jewellery. For

SEMI-PRECIOUS BEADS

1. *Aquamarine chips* **2.** *Opalite chips* **3.** *7 mm (⁵⁄₁₆ in) round turquoise beads* **4.** *Assorted florite beads* **5.** *Assorted amethyst beads* **6.** *1 cm (³⁄₈ in) round rutilated quartz beads* **7.** *Florite tumble beads* **8.** *Lapis raw tumble beads* **9.** *Brown sandstone chips* **10.** *8 x 6 mm (⁵⁄₁₆ x ¼ in) facetted labrodite brick beads* **11.** *Citrine chips* **12.** *Pressed coral chips* **13.** *1 cm (³⁄₈ in) chalcedony smooth tumble beads* **14.** *4 mm (¹⁄₆ in) round carnelian beads* **15.** *Apatite smooth chips* **16.** *Rock crystal broad bean beads* **17.** *2 x 1.2 cm (¾ x ½ in) facetted flat rectangle cherry quartz beads* **18.** *Tumble rose quartz beads* **19.** *2 cm (¾ in) hematite rectangular beads* **20.** *5 mm (¼ in) peridot triangular beads*

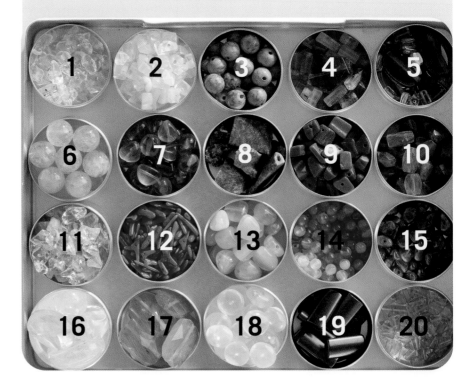

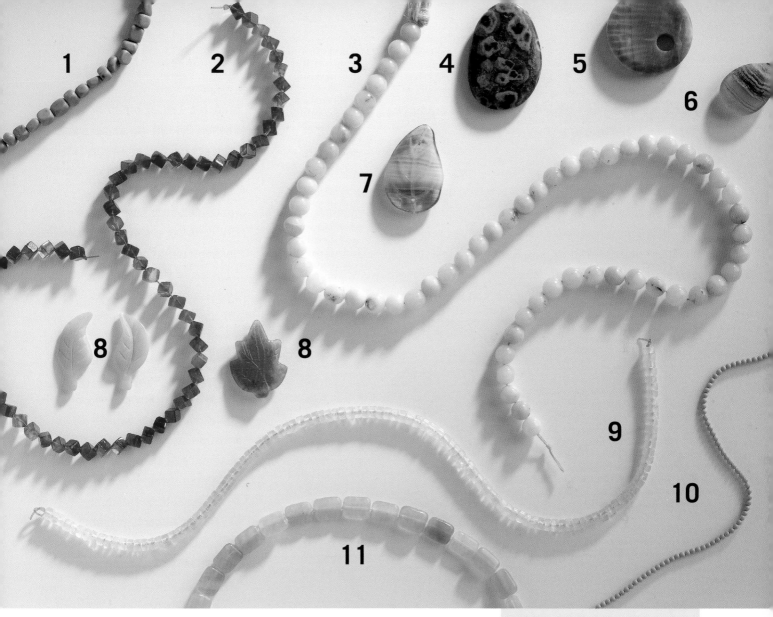

instance, calcite eases back pain, coral alleviates teething and rose quartz heals a broken heart.

The shine of semi-precious stone can be dulled by perfume and natural body oil. Polish semi-precious jewellery with a dry cloth. If necessary, soak the jewellery in luke-warm water with a gentle anti-bacterial dish washing soap. Rinse, then pat the jewellery dry.

Bead strings and feature beads

Most semi-precious beads are available strung rather than loose. Some come on silk cord ready to be made into necklaces or bracelets. Distinctive feature beads are sold individually and are great to use as pendants.

Keep the rest of a necklace or bracelet understated to display a feature bead to best effect.

BEAD STRINGS AND FEATURE BEADS

1. *6 mm (¼ in) square turquoise beads*

2. *4 mm (⅙ in) square carnelian beads*

3. *7 mm (⁵⁄₁₆ in) round pink opal beads*

4. *Agate side drilled oval bead*

5. *Fire agate agogo pendant*

6. *Amethyst side drilled bead*

7. *Moonstone pendant* **8.** *Dyed jade carved leaves* **9.** *6 mm (¼ in) flat round pink quartz beads* **10.** *2 mm (¹⁄₁₀ in) round turquoise beads*

11. *1 cm x 8 mm (⅜ x ⁵⁄₁₆ in) rectangular blue calcite beads*

THREADING MATERIAL

Beads can be strung on a variety of threading materials. The size of the hole in the bead often determines the threading material. Many freshwater pearls have very small holes. This is because they are sold in bulk by weight and the smaller the hole, the heavier the bead! Therefore,

use a fine bead cord or thread such as Nymo with the finest beading needle. Beads with large holes can be threaded on thonging and ribbon or suspended on ballpins and headpins.

Make bracelets and necklaces any length you wish. Here are standard finished lengths:

Bracelet: 18–20 cm (7–8 in)
Choker: 33–38 cm (13–15 in)
Princess necklace: 45 cm (18 in)
Matinee necklace: 60 cm (24 in)

(1) Carded bead cord: this twisted silk cord has a stainless steel needle fixed to one end. The cord comes in different thicknesses and lots of colours.

(2) Flexible beading wire: fine wires are twisted together and nylon coated to make this strong wire. The more strands of wire, the more flexible the wire. Seven-strand, 19-strand and 49-strand wires are available. All come in different thicknesses and a range of colours. Nineteen-strand is the most versatile of the range.

(3) Fine bead cord: available on a reel, this synthetic twisted cord is extremely strong and will not stretch.

(4) Nymo thread: this is a strong nylon thread that comes in a large choice of colours. Use Nymo for stringing small beads and bead weaving.

(5) Quilting thread: although not a usual beading thread, this strong thread is economical to use when a large quantity of thread is needed, for a bead loom project for example. Run the thread over beeswax to stop it tangling.

(6) Cord thonging and (7) ribbon: consider other materials to thread beads onto. A simple necklace of

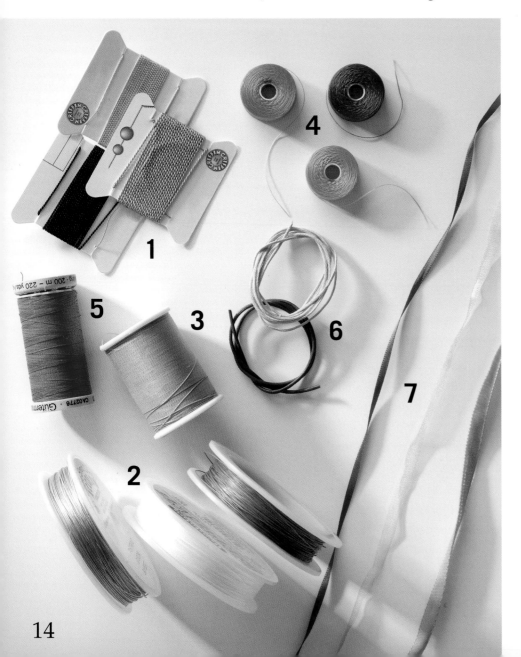

cotton or leather cord or ribbon will set off a pendant beautifully.

(8) Wire: use sterling silver or gold-filled wire with semi-precious beads. The thickness of wire is measured in gauges; the higher the number, the thinner the wire.

(9) 26 gauge (0.4 mm) wire: this size wire is useful for making findings and twisting together.

(10) 18 gauge (1 mm) half hard wire: bend this wire with pliers to make pendants and rings. The wire can be filed with a jewellery file or a metal manicure file.

(11) Memory wire: also known as remembrance wire, this coiled wire always returns to its original shape. Use memory wire shears or strong wire snippers to cut the wire. The wire comes in three sizes that are suitable for making rings, bracelets and choker necklaces. To finish and stop beads slipping off, bend the wire back on itself or glue on a stop bead at each end.

(12) Gimp: also known as French wire and bullion, gimp is a narrow tube of twisted wire. Use gimp to cover and protect bead cord from rubbing against a clasp.

(13) Chain: is available by the metre (yard) and is often sold in convenient half-metre lengths. Fix beads to chain with headpins, ballpins, eye pins or jump rings.

FINDINGS

Findings are the metal components that turn your beaded creations into jewellery. Do justice to your semi-precious beads by using good quality sterling silver, gold-filled and vermeil findings. Silver is too soft to be durable alone so a little of another metal, usually copper, is added to increase its hardness. To be defined as silver, it must have 92.5 per cent silver, as does sterling silver. Gold-filled findings are a realistic alternative to the more expensive real gold. Gold filled means that a solid layer of gold has been bonded to a base metal, which is often brass. Vermeil has a sterling silver base coated with gold.

(1) Headpins and (2) ballpins: headpins resemble long dressmaking pins whilst ballpins have a small, distinctive ball at the end. Both are available in different lengths. 3.5 cm (1⅜ in) and 5 cm (2 in) lengths are the most versatile and are used in the projects in this book. A bead or beads are threaded onto the pin and a loop made above for hanging.

(3) Eye pins: eye pins have a loop (this is the eye) at one end. Use eye pins for pinning beads or to fix the ends of strings of beads to, the eye is then hidden in an end cap. You can make your own eye pin by turning a loop at the end of a length of wire.

(4) Jump rings: these small rings join components together. Jump rings come in different sizes and they are usually round, but oval jump rings are also available. Join a row of jump rings together to make a chain.

(5) Closed rings: a closed ring does not open so anything that is suspended from it needs to open. A fixed ring can be a feature of a piece of jewellery.

(6) Crimp beads: these tiny metal cylinders are squeezed closed to secure the ends of beading wire to a clasp or other component. Fix crimp beads with a pair of crimping pliers.

(7) End bars: finish a multi-strand necklace or bracelet with a pair of end bars to separate the bead strings. They come in various styles with different numbers of holes for fixing the strings of beads to. Some necklace clasps incorporate end bars.

(8) Spacer bars: spacer bars have a row of drilled holes to separate strings of beads. Use spacer bars that co-ordinate with end bars.

(9) End caps: also called bell caps, these caps will conceal the ends of multi-strand necklaces or bracelets to create a neat finish.

(10) Calotte crimps: finish necklaces or bracelets strung on bead string or thread with calotte crimps which have two hinged cups to hide the knotted end of strung beads.

(11) Necklace clasps: there is a beautiful and versatile range of necklace clasps available to fasten necklaces and bracelets.

(12) Extension chain: use an extension chain to lengthen a necklace. A bead can be fixed to the end of the chain to co-ordinate with the necklace.

(13) Cord ends: the ends of thick cord are dabbed with glue and inserted into a cord end which is then squeezed closed with a pair of snipe-nose pliers to hold the cord. A hole at the end of the cord end is fixed to a necklace clasp.

(14) Earring wires: hang beaded pieces on ear studs or fish hooks which have a loop below to suspend beaded pieces from. Ear clips are also available for unpierced ears. Hoops come in different sizes and are great for making flamboyant gypsy style earrings.

(15) Sieves and backs: sieves are perforated discs that beads can be sewn to with wire or have beads on headpins or ballpins fixed to. The sieves are then fixed with small prongs to a brooch, ear clip or ring back.

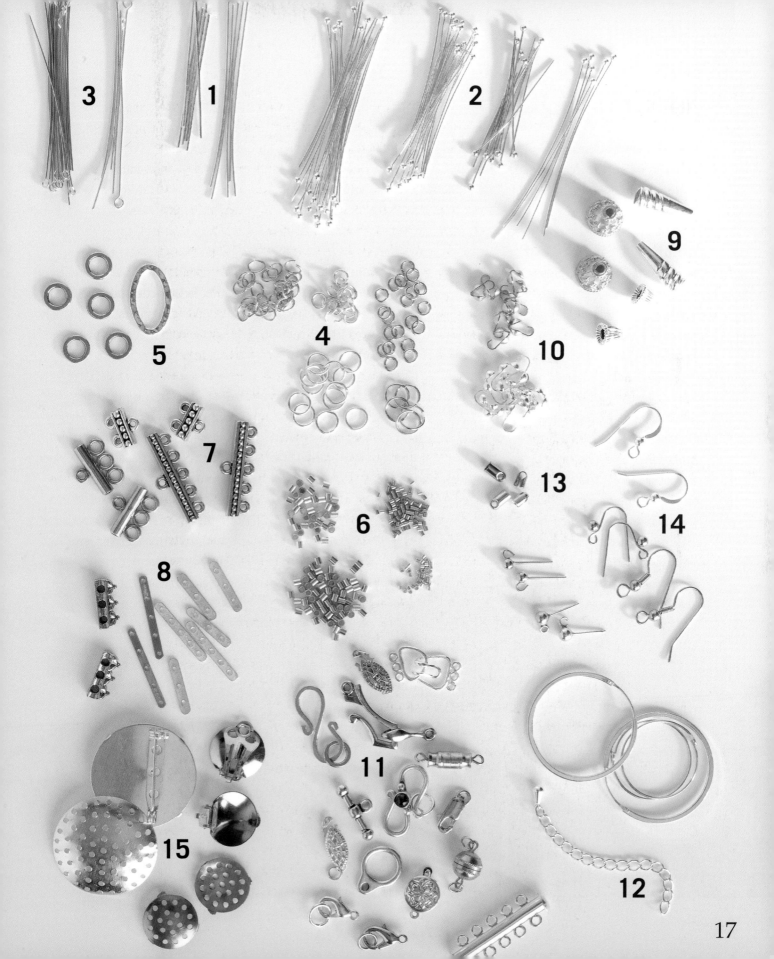

TECHNIQUES

The techniques described in this section are used throughout the book. Before embarking on a project, read the instructions carefully to check that you are familiar with the techniques used. Always follow metric or imperial measurements, but never a combination of both.

MAKING A SINGLE LOOP

Beads attached to ballpins and headpins can be hung from a chain or a pair of earrings to create jewellery in an instant. The closer to the tip of the jaws of a pair of round-nose pliers that you hold the wire, the smaller the loop will be. Therefore, the further up the jaws you hold the wire, the larger the loop. To make beads with single loops of a uniform size, always hold the wire at the same position. A small strip of masking tape wrapped around one jaw can act as a guide for positioning the loop.

1 Slip a bead or beads onto a ballpin, headpin or eyepin. Start with a small bead if the other bead holes are large and prone to slip off the ball of a ballpin or the head of a headpin. Cut off the excess wire 7 mm (5⁄16 in) above the last bead with wire snippers. Leave a longer length of wire if you want to make a larger loop.

2 Hold the end of the wire with a pair of round-nose pliers. Bend the wire away from you at a right angle on top of the last bead.

3 Turn your wrist to curl the wire towards you as far as is comfortable to make a loop. Release the wire and grab it again to continue rolling it into a loop. It should resemble a closed circle. If you wish, apply a dab of cyanoacrylate adhesive, jeweller's cement or clear nail varnish on the join to secure the loop.

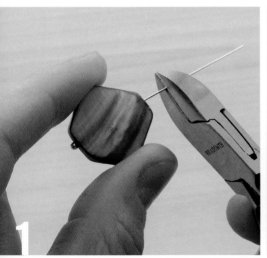

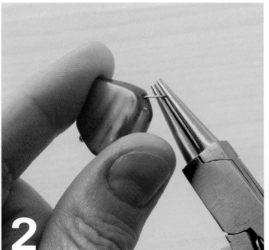

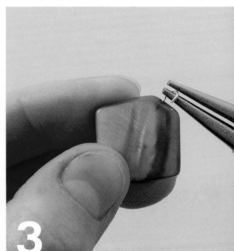

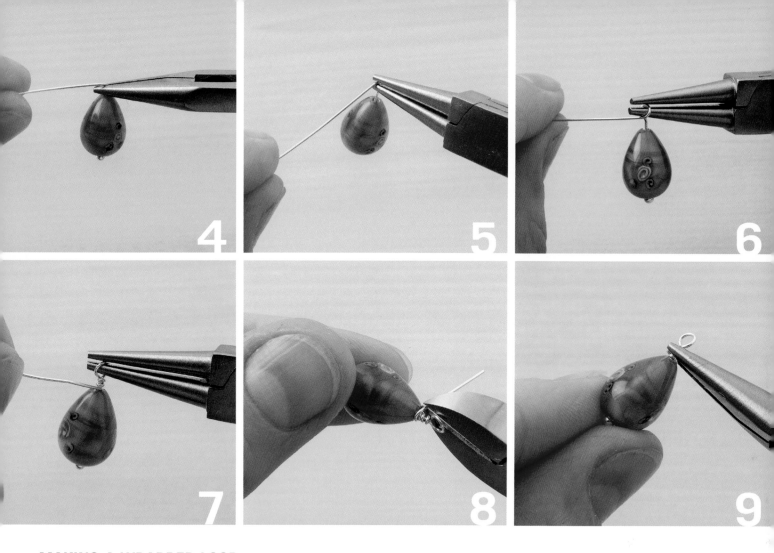

MAKING A WRAPPED LOOP

A wrapped loop is securely closed so is suitable for heavy beads. It is easier to wrap with a fine wire but use thick wire on heavy beads.

4 Slip a bead or beads onto a ballpin or headpin. Start with a small bead if the other bead holes are large and prone to slip off the ball of a ballpin or the head of a headpin. Hold the wire with the tips of a pair of snipe-nose pliers, resting the jaws on the last bead. Using your fingers, bend the wire over the jaws at a right angle.

5 Hold the wire with a pair of round-nose pliers close to the bend in the wire. Roll the wire over the jaw of the pliers towards you as far as is comfortable to make a loop.

6 Release the wire and grab it again to continue rolling it into a loop, ending up with the wire again at right angles to the wire coming from the bead.

7 With the round-nose pliers slipped through the loop to hold the wire steady, wrap the extending wire neatly around the wire coming from the bead.

8 Snip off the excess wire close to the bead.

9 Squeeze the snipped end close to the wrapped wire with a pair of snipe-nose pliers.

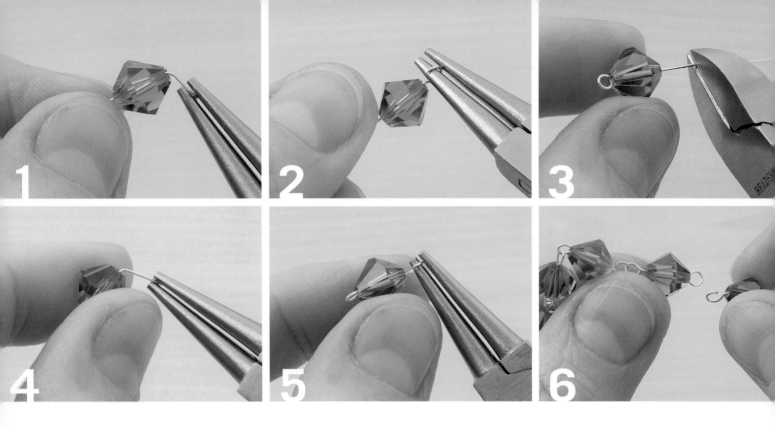

PINNING BEADS

Pinned beads are threaded onto wire or an eye pin and will have a loop at each side. The loops (eyes) can be joined together to make a length of pinned beads. If you are using a eye pin, start at Step 3. If you intend to make a number of pinned beads, wrap a small strip of masking tape around one jaw of a pair of round-nose pliers to mark the place to hold the wire when making the loop. This will ensure that the loops are all the same size.

1 Thread a bead or beads onto a length of 26-gauge (0.4 mm) wire. Bend 7 mm (⁵⁄₁₆ in) at one end of the wire with a pair of round-nose pliers away from you at a right angle over the pliers.

2 Hold the end of the wire with a pair of round-nose pliers. Turn your wrist to curl the wire towards you as far as is comfortable to make a loop. Release the wire and grab it again to continue rolling it into a loop.

3 Slip the beads down the wire to the loop. Cut off the excess wire 7 mm (⁵⁄₁₆ in) above the last bead with wire snippers.

4 Hold the end of the wire with a pair of round-nose pliers. Bend the wire away from you at a right angle on top of the last bead.

5 Turn your wrist to curl the wire towards you as far as is comfortable to start to form the loop. Release the wire and grab it again to continue rolling it into a loop.

6 To attach pinned beads together, use a pair of round-nose pliers to lift one loop open. If you are opening a loop on thicker wire, such as an eye pin, slip a closed loop or jump ring onto the open loop and then use two pairs of pliers to close it. If you wish, apply a dab of cyanoacrylate adhesive, jeweller's cement or clear nail varnish on the join to secure the loop.

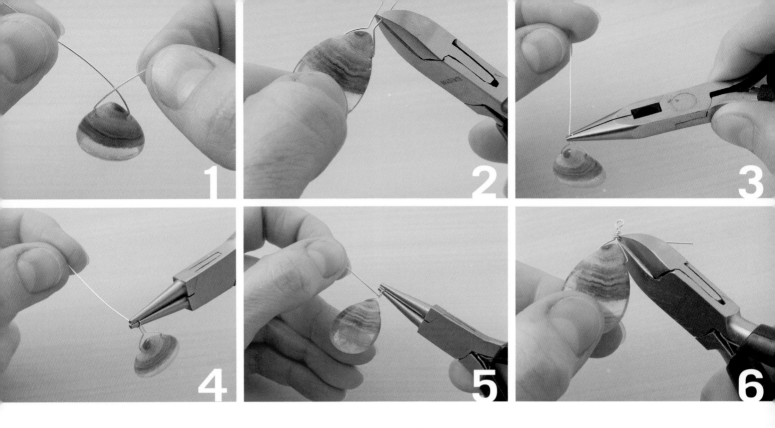

MAKING A WRAPPED SIDE OR TOP DRILLED BEAD

Use this method to fix a side drilled bead with a side drilled hole onto wire. Making a wrapped loop above the bead will secure it in place.

1 Slip a side drilled bead onto an 8 cm (3¼ in) length of 26-gauge (0.4 mm) wire with 2 cm (¾ in) of the wire extending at one side. Pull the wires tightly across the top of the bead.

2 Use a pair of snipe-nose pliers to bend each wire upwards at the point where the two wires cross. Snip the short end of wire 3 mm (⅛ in) above the top of the bead with wire snippers.

3 Hold the wires with a pair of snipe-nose pliers, resting the jaws on the bead. Bend the extending wire over the jaws at a right angle.

4 Make a loop above the bend in the wire using a pair of round-nose pliers, ending up with the wire again at right angles to the wire coming from the bead.

5 With the round-nose pliers slipped through the loop to hold the wire steady, wrap the extending wire neatly around both wires coming from the bead.

6 Snip off the excess wire close to the bead. Squeeze the snipped end close to the wrapped wire with a pair of snipe-nose pliers.

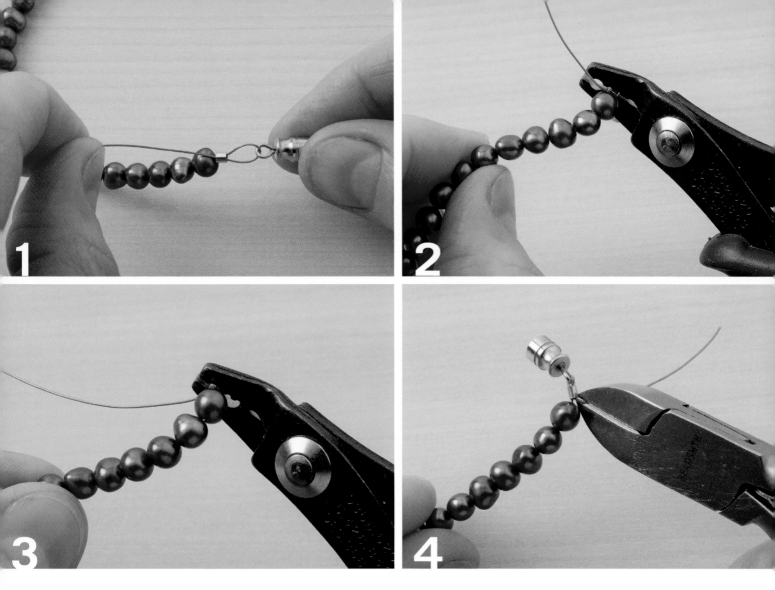

USING A CRIMP BEAD

Crimp beads resemble small metal beads. They are easy to fix in place with a pair of crimping pliers but a pair of snipe-nose pliers will suffice to flatten the crimp but will not give the neat, rounded shape achieved with crimping pliers.

1 Slip a crimp bead onto flexible beading wire, usually after beads for a necklace or bracelet. Thread on a necklace clasp, jump ring or other jewellery component. Pull the end of the beading wire back through the crimp bead, leaving a small loop of beading wire around the component but loose enough to allow for some movement.

2 Place the crimp bead in the inner notch of a pair of crimping pliers. Squeeze the pliers

closed. The squashed crimp will be crescent shaped.

3 Now, place the crimp bead in the outer notch of the pliers. Squeeze the pliers closed. This will round the shape of the crimp. Release and turn the crimp in the notch and close the pliers again to improve the shape.

4 Snip off the excess beading wire as close as possible to the crimp with wire snippers.

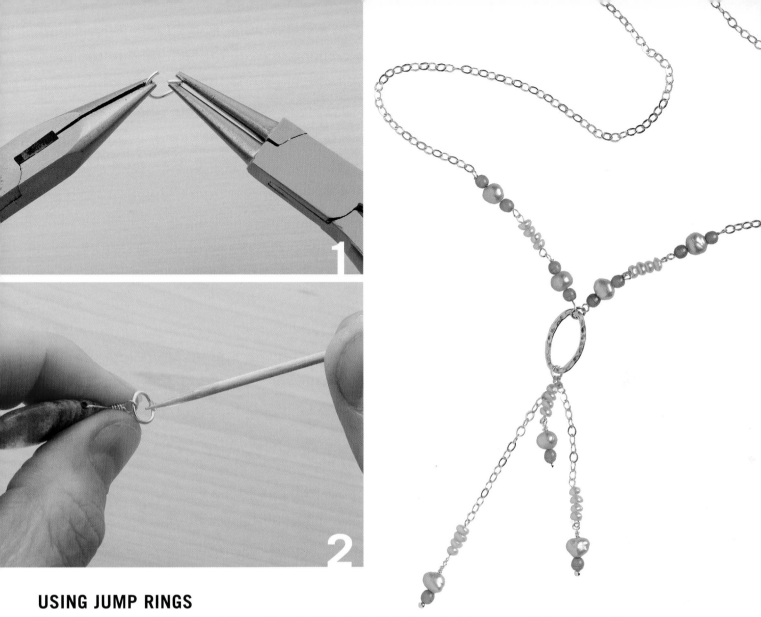

USING JUMP RINGS

Jump rings are used throughout the projects in this book. It is important to open and close jump rings sideways. Do not pull jump rings open outwards as they will weaken and may snap.

1 Hold the jump ring with a pair of pliers on one side of the opening and another pair of pliers on the other side of the opening. For instance, use a pair of snipe-nose and a pair of round-nose pliers. Open the jump ring by gently pulling one pair of pliers towards you until the opening is large enough to slip your jewellery component onto.

2 Push the same pair of pliers away from you to close the jump ring, making sure the opening is realigned. For extra security, dab the opening with cyanoacrylate adhesive, jeweller's cement or clear nail varnish. Use the tip of a cocktail stick to deliver a tiny amount of adhesive or nail varnish.

PROJECTS

Memory wire ring

Memory wire is a stiff, spring-like wire that returns to its tightly coiled form when it is expanded and released. This memory wire ring is threaded with sparkling crystals and dotted with silver stars. Make a few rings in contrasting colours for maximum drama.

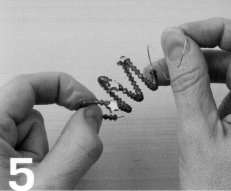

YOU WILL NEED

Silver plated ring memory wire

Memory wire shears
  or strong wire snippers

Round-nose pliers

76 x 3 mm (⅛ in) indicolite
  bicone crystal beads

3 sterling silver 6 mm (¼ in)
  star beads

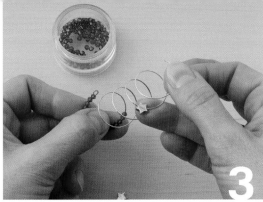

VARIATION: This simple memory wire ring is threaded with eighty-two 3 mm (⅛ in) bicone crystals in pretty shades of pink and purple.

1 Separate five coils from the main body of the silver plated ring memory wire. Snip off coils using memory wire shears or strong wire snippers. Bend one end of the wire into a small loop with the tips of a pair of round-nose pliers. It is important to bend memory wire in the opposite direction to its natural curve.

2 Pull open the coils and thread on seventeen 3 mm (⅛ in) indicolite bicone crystal beads. Slip the crystal beads along the wire to the loop.

3 Thread on a sterling silver star bead. Thread on twenty-two crystal beads.

4 Thread on a sterling silver star bead. Thread on twenty-one crystal beads and another star bead.

5 Thread on sixteen crystal beads. Move the crystal beads and stars along the wire to butt up against the loop. Snip the wire 1.2 cm (½ in) after the last crystal bead.

6 Bend the end of the wire into a small loop with the tips of a pair of round-nose pliers, remembering to bend the memory wire in the opposite direction to its natural curve.

TIP:
Memory wire is very strong. Do not use ordinary jewellery pliers to cut it. Always use memory wire shears or strong wire snippers.

27

Three-strand bracelet

Semi-precious chips are inexpensive and their irregular shapes suit the rustic handcrafted look of Bali-style silver beads and findings. This bracelet features an unusual Bali-style bead at the centre which anchors three strands of delicately coloured aquamarine chips.

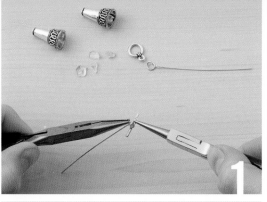

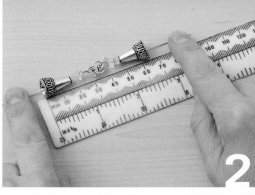

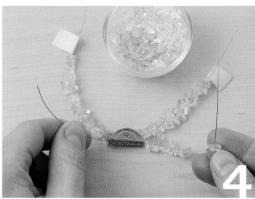

YOU WILL NEED

2 sterling silver eye pins

2 sterling silver 4 mm (⅙ in)
jump rings

Snipe-nose pliers

Round-nose pliers

1 sterling silver hoop and bar
necklace clasp

Pair of 1 cm (⅜ in) sterling silver
end caps

1 string of aquamarine chips

Wire snippers

90 cm (36 in) flexible
beading wire

1.2 cm (½ in) Bali style sterling
silver filigree flattened round bead

Masking tape

6 x 1 mm (¹⁄₁₆ in) crimp beads

Crimping pliers

1 To calculate the length of the bracelet, slip the eye of each eye pin onto a 4 mm (⅙ in) jump ring. Fix the jump rings onto the ring at each side of a hoop and bar necklace clasp using a pair of snipe-nose and round-nose pliers. Fasten the necklace clasp. Thread two chips and an end cap onto each eye pin.

2 Lay the piece flat and measure the length. For the final measurement, subtract this measurement from the desired bracelet length. Use wire snippers to snip three lengths of flexible beading wire 8 cm (3¼ in) longer than the final measurement. Remove the eye pins and set the four chips and end caps aside.

3 Thread a 1.2 cm (½ in) Bali style sterling silver filigree flattened round bead onto the centre of one length of flexible beading wire. Thread aquamarine chips onto each end of the beading wire leaving 4 cm (1⅝ in) at each end. Wrap a piece of masking tape around the ends to stop the chips sliding off.

4 Slip the second length of beading wire through the silver bead and thread chips on each end and tape the ends as before. Repeat with the third length of beading wire.

5

6

7

8

9

VARIATION: Here is a neat bracelet of three strands of sterling silver beads, red glass rocaille beads and 4 mm (⅙ in) garnet beads.

5 Peel the tape off the end of one length of beading wire, thread on a crimp bead and eye pin. Insert the beading wire back through the crimp bead, leave a small loop of beading wire through the eye pin that allows for some movement.

6 Refer to the **Using a crimp bead technique** on page 22 to fix the crimp bead in place using a pair of crimping pliers. Snip off the excess beading wire with wire snippers. Repeat to fix the other end to an eye pin with a crimp bead.

7 Fix the remaining lengths of threaded beading wire to the eye pins in the same way.

8 Thread an end cap onto one eye pin. It will cover the crimped ends of the beading wire. Thread on two aquamarine chips. Refer to the **Making a wrapped loop technique** on page 19 to make a wrapped loop above the chips. Repeat on the other end of the bracelet.

9 Use a a pair of snipe-nose and round-nose pliers to open a jump ring on the necklace clasp. Slip the loop of one wrapped loop onto the jump ring. Close the jump ring using the pliers. Repeat at the other end of the necklace clasp.

Two-way necklace

This pretty necklace is very versatile. It can be slipped over the head and worn as a single long length or worn as a double shorter length that fastens at the front. Choose an attractive hoop and bar necklace fastening as it will be a feature of the necklace. The hoop suspends some choice beads, add as many as you wish.

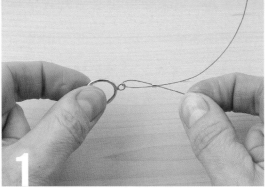

1 Snip a 45 cm (18 in) length of flexible beading wire with a pair of wire snippers. Slip a crimp bead then the ring of a 1.6 cm (⅝ in) vermeil hoop necklace fastening onto one end. Insert the end of the beading wire through the crimp bead, suspending the hoop.

2 Secure the crimp bead using a pair of crimping pliers, referring to the **Using a crimp bead technique** on page 22. Snip off the excess beading wire with wire snippers.

3 Set aside a freshwater pearl from each string of pearls. Thread one string of pearls onto the beading wire.

4 Slip on a crimp bead and the ring of the bar of the necklace clasp. Insert the end of the beading wire through the crimp bead, suspending the bar.

5 Secure the crimp bead using a pair of crimping pliers as before. Snip off the excess beading wire with wire snippers. Repeat Steps 1 to 5 to fix a second string of pearls between the necklace clasp.

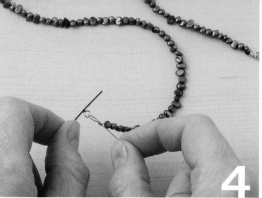

3

4

5

8

6 Slip a 1.8 cm (1¹⁄₁₆ in) light blue drop lamp bead and one of the remaining pearls onto a 3.5 cm (1⅜ in) gold-filled ballpin. Refer to the **Making a wrapped loop technique** on page 19 to fix the bead and pearl in place using a pair of snipe-nose and round-nose pliers. Fix an 8 mm (⁵⁄₁₆ in) padparadscha drop crystal to a ballpin with a wrapped loop in the same way.

7 Slip a mother-of-pearl chip, a rose quartz chip, the remaining pearl and a 4 mm (⅙ in) light azore bicone crystal onto a ball pin. Slip a 6 mm (¼ in) light colarado facetted rondel, a 4 mm (⅙ in) light azore bicone crystal and a 3 mm (⅛ in) rose alabaster bicone crystal onto a ballpin. Fix in place with a wrapped loop.

8 Use the pliers to open five 7 x 5 mm (⁵⁄₃₂ x ¼ in) gold-filled oval jump rings. Slip the loop of one of the wrapped loops and the hoop of the necklace clasp onto one jump ring. Close the jump ring securely using both pairs of pliers. Fix the remaining fixed loops and a fuschia crystal pendant to the hoop in the same way. Carefully apply a little cyanoacrylate adhesive or jeweller's cement to the join of the jump rings to secure them closed.

VARIATION: Coral freshwater pearls are used with sterling silver findings on this two-way necklace. The hoop clasp suspends a silver heart charm, glass, pearl and crystal beads.

33

Flower drop earrings

Delicate flowers carved from glass or semi-precious stones are suspended below mother-of-pearl beads on these pretty earrings. They are simple to make and would be a lovely gift for a bride or bridesmaid. The flowers can hang on as many mother-of-pearl beads as you wish. Here, pink cats-eye flowers hang are teamed with nine mother-of-pearl beads.

YOU WILL NEED

40 cm (16 in) flexible beading wire

Wire snippers

2 x 1.5 cm (⅝ in) pink cats-eye (glass) carved flowers with centre hole

18 x 4 mm (⅙ in) mother-of-pearl beads

2 x gold-filled crimp beads

Pair of gold-filled fish hook earring wires

Crimping pliers

1 Thread a 1.5 cm (⅝ in) pink cats-eye (glass) carved flower with a centre hole onto a 20 cm (8 in) length of flexible beading wire. Slip the flower along the beading wire to the centre.

2 Bring the ends of the beading wire together and thread on nine 4 mm (⅙ in) mother-of-pearl beads. Thread on fewer beads if you prefer a shorter drop.

3 Insert the ends of the beading wire through a crimp bead and the eye of a fish hook earring wire.

4 Pull the ends of the beading wire to tighten the loop around the earring wire but allow some room for movement. Adjust the flower to face forward as you tighten the beading wire.

5 Secure the crimp bead using a pair of crimping pliers, referring to the **Using a crimp bead technique** on page 22.

6 Snip off the excess beading wire close to the crimp bead with wire snippers. Make a matching earring.

VARIATION: Dazzling violet crystal flowers hang below ten 3 mm (⅛ in) bicone crystals on these glamourous earrings.

Bound bangle

This twinkling, chunky bangle studded with sequins and crystals started life as a humble wooden bangle. The bangle is bound with pale gold rocaille beads with sequins and crystals applied at random.

YOU WILL NEED

Short beading needle

Quilting thread

Wooden or plastic bangle

Cyanoacrylate adhesive

40g of size 11 pale gold glass rocaille beads

Masking tape

Approx. 48 gold cup sequins

Approx. 48 x 4 mm (⅙ in) bicone crystal beads in shades of green, turquoise and brown

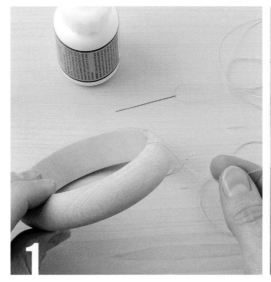

1 Thread a short beading needle with a 150 cm (60 in) double length of quilting thread. Knot the ends together. Slip the needle through the middle of the bangle and insert the needle between the threads. Pull the threads tight and glue the knot to the inside of the bangle.

2 Thread on about fifty rocaille beads. Slip the beads down the thread to the knot. Wrap the bead strung thread around the bangle. Stick a piece of masking tape inside the bangle to hold the strung beads in place.

3 Continue threading on beads. Wrap the beaded thread tightly around the bangle until there are one and a half rows of beads on the outside of the bangle. Insert the needle up through a cup sequin then thread on a bicone crystal bead.

4 Insert the needle back through the sequin. Pull the thread so that the sequin rests on the last rocaille bead with the crystal bead on the centre of the sequin.

5 Now insert the needle through the last rocaille bead, towards the free end of thread.

6 Continue threading on beads and wrapping them closely around the bangle, applying a sequin and crystal bead on the outside of the bangle on alternate rows of beads. Push the rows together so that they cover the bangle. Use masking tape inside the bangle to keep the strung beads together.

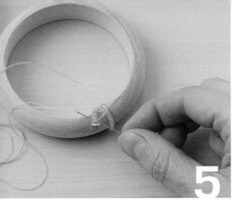

5

6

7

10

VARIATION: This technique is effective without the sequins and crystals as shown on this narrow bangle bound with shiny red glass rocaille beads.

7 When the beads are about 15 cm (6 in) from the end of the thread, cut off the needle. Bind the thread twice around the bangle and glue in place. Cut off the excess thread.

8 Thread the needle with a 150 cm (60 in) double length of quilting thread and knot the ends together. Slip the needle through the middle of the bangle and insert the needle between the threads as before. Pull the threads tight and glue the knot to the inside of the bangle close to the beading. Insert the needle through the last six beads.

9 Continue beading the bangle, finishing and adding more thread when necessary as described in Steps 7 to 8.

10 Insert the needle through the first six beads. Part the beads and bind the thread a few times around the bangle. Carefully glue the threads to the bangle. Cut off the excess thread.

TIP:
Use a bangle similar in colour to the rocaille beads. Remember that the bangle will be a tighter fit once it has been beaded.

Rosette cuff

This unusual cuff is made up of sparkling beaded rosettes. The glass bead at the centre of each rosette is circled with delicately woven delica beads. The rosettes are joined together and fastened with a beaded loop and glass bead 'button'.

YOU WILL NEED

Nymo thread

Short beading needle

Approx. 19 x 1.2 mm (½ in) green foil lined disc glass beads

20 g of green delica beads

1 Thread a 75 cm (29½ in) length of Nymo thread onto a short beading needle. Thread the needle through a green foil lined disc glass bead, leaving a 20 cm (8 in) trailing length of thread. Insert the needle through the disc bead again then repeat, adjusting the threads so that they are on opposite sides of the rim of the bead.

2 Thread on two delica beads. Slip the beads down the thread to rest on the disc bead.

TIP
Measure your wrist, allowing room for movement. Subtract 1.8 cm (¾ in) from the measurement to allow for the button and loop fastening. Make the strip of rosettes in Step 8 the length of the resulting measurement.

3 Holding the trailing end of thread so that the threads are taut, insert the needle under the first thread.

4 Now insert the needle back up through the last delica bead. Pull the thread so that the delica bead rests on the disc bead. Thread on one delica bead. Repeat Steps 3 to 4 until you have covered the first half of the disc bead.

5 Continue in the same way around the second half of the disc bead. Insert the needle down through the first delica bead then up through the last delica bead to complete the first ring of beads.

6 Thread on two delica beads to start the second ring of beads. Insert the needle under the

thread that is on top of the first ring of beads. Insert the needle up through the second delica bead.

7 Thread on one delica bead. Repeat Step 5 to apply the second ring of beads. Insert the needle down through the first delica bead of the second ring of beads, then up through the last delica bead to complete the second ring of beads. Apply the third ring of delica beads in the same way as the second ring of beads.

8 Make nine rosettes of three rings of beads and nine rosettes of two rings of beads. Leave the ends of threads trailing. To form the cuff, arrange the rosettes touching edge to edge, two deep in a row with a rosette of two rings at each end.

9 Starting at one end of the cuff, join the rosettes together using the trailing ends of threads by weaving the threads between two beads that are side by side on the outer rings where the rosettes butt together. Work the threads through the beadwork and cut off the excess, leaving a thread trailing from the rosette at each end of the cuff.

10 To make a disc glass bead 'button' thread a disc bead then four delica beads onto the thread at one end of the cuff. Slip the beads down the thread. Insert the needle back through the first delica bead and the disc bead.

VARIATION: A purple foil-lined glass bead has been circled with woven rings of metallic delica beads. The loop at the top means that it can be suspended as a pendant from a length of fine organza ribbon.

11 Insert the needle through the next delica bead on the outer ring. Insert the needle through the delica bead where it first emerged to make the button. Repeat Steps 10 to 11 to secure the button then weave the thread through the beadwork and cut off the excess.

12 Thread enough delica beads onto the thread at the other end of the cuff to loop around the button. Insert the needle through the next bead on the outer ring to make the loop. Insert the needle through the delica bead where it first emerged. Repeat to secure the loop then weave the thread through the beadwork and cut off the excess.

Ribbon tied necklace

An eclectic mixture of components and textures are combined to create this fabulous necklace in shades of green. The beautiful deep green dyed mother-of-pearl polos have a side drilled hole which makes them very versatile to use. Bias cut ribbon is an unusual addition to the necklace.

YOU WILL NEED

120 cm (48 in) flexible beading wire

Wire snippers

17 gold-filled crimp beads

7 x 2 cm (¾ in) dyed deep green side drilled mother-of-pearl polos

Crimping pliers

15 x 6 mm (¼ in) olive jade rondel beads

11 x 1.8 cm (¾ in) lime / turquoise glass coin beads

2 olive jade carved leaves

80 cm (31 in) of 1.5 cm (⅝ in) wide bias ribbon

Sewing scissors

2 x 8 mm (⁵⁄₁₆ in) vermeil closed rings

2 x 7 x 5 mm (⁵⁄₃₂ x ¼ in) gold-filled oval jump rings

Snipe-nose pliers

Round-nose pliers

1 x vermeil necklace clasp

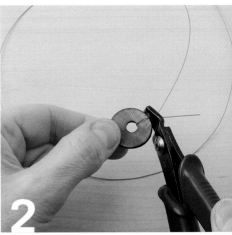

1 Snip a 50 cm (20 in) length of flexible beading wire with a pair of wire snippers. Thread a crimp bead onto one end. Insert one end of the beading wire through the centre of a polo. Thread the end of the beading wire back through the crimp bead, suspending the polo.

2 Slip the crimp bead along the beading wire to rest against the polo. Secure the crimp bead using a pair of crimping pliers, referring to the **Using a crimp bead technique** on page 22. Snip off the excess beading wire with wire snippers.

TIP
You may need seven large crimp beads to accommodate the two thicknesses of flexible beading wire, and ten small crimp beads to neaten the single extending ends of beading wire as the large size may slip off the single beading wire.

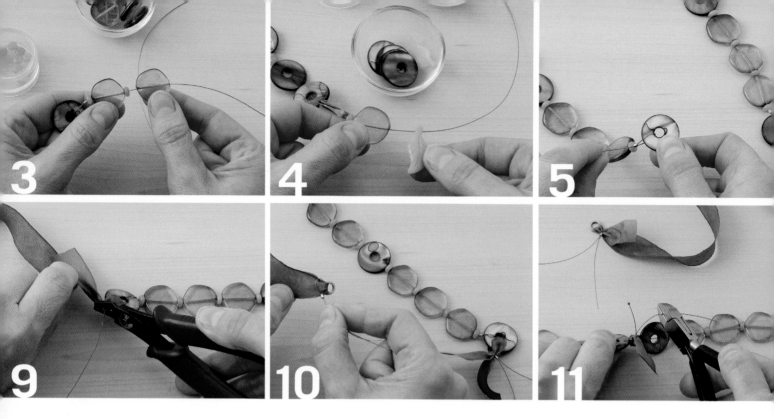

3 Thread on a 6 mm (¼ in) olive jade rondel bead and a 1.8 cm (¾ in) lime / turquoise glass coin bead. Repeat twice. Thread on a rondel bead.

4 Insert the beading wire through a polo, two rondel beads, two polos, one rondel, one coin bead, one rondel, one coin bead, one carved leaf, one coin bead, one carved leaf, one polo, one rondel, one coin, one rondel, one coin, one rondel and one polo. Repeat Step 3.

5 Thread on a crimp bead. Insert the beading wire through the centre of a polo. Thread the end of the beading wire back through the crimp bead, suspending the polo. Slip the crimp along the beading wire

to rest between the rondel and the polo. Secure the crimp bead using a pair of crimping pliers, referring to the **Using a crimp bead technique** on page 22. Snip off the excess beading wire with wire snippers.

6 Snip five 12.5 cm (4 in) lengths of beading wire with wire snippers. Bend the beading wire in half and insert the ends through a crimp bead. Cut a 14 cm (5½ in) length of ribbon with a pair of scissors. Fold the ribbon around the pair of rondel beads.

7 Slip one of the beading wire loops over the ends of the ribbon. Slip the crimp bead along the beading wire to tighten the loop around the ribbon. Fix

the crimp bead in place with a pair of crimping pliers. Trim the ends of the ribbon with a pair of sewing scissors.

8 Cut two 30 cm (12 in) lengths of ribbon. Slip the end of one ribbon through one beading wire loop. Thread 5 cm (2 in) at the end of the ribbon through the centre of a polo then through the beading wire loop.

9 Slip the crimp bead along the flexible beading wire and tighten the loop around the ribbon close to the polo. Fix the crimp bead in place with a pair of crimping pliers. Trim the short end of the ribbon with a pair of sewing scissors. Repeat on the polo at the other end of the necklace.

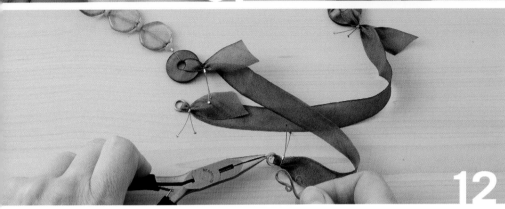

10 Slip the raw end of one ribbon through one beading wire loop. Thread 5 cm (2 in) of ribbon through the centre of an 8 mm (5/16 in) vermeil closed ring then through the beading wire loop. Slip the crimp bead along the beading wire to loop it tightly around the ribbon close to the closed ring. Fix the crimp bead in place with a pair of crimping pliers. Trim the short end of the ribbon with a pair of sewing scissors. Repeat on the other ribbon.

11 Slip a crimp bead onto each extending end of beading wire. Fix the crimp 2 cm (3/4 in) from the first crimped beads with crimping pliers. Snip off the end of beading wire with wire snippers close to the crimped beads.

12 Open a 7 x 5 mm (5/32 x 1/4 in) gold-filled oval jump ring with a pair of snipe-nose and round-nose pliers. Slip the jump ring onto the closed ring and the vermeil necklace clasp. Close the jump ring using the pliers. Repeat at the other end of the necklace.

VARIATION: Shades of pink have been used on this stunning necklace. Rose quartz rondel beads are interspersed between dyed magenta mother-of-pearl polos and square foil lined glass beads. Note that a rondel bead each side of the carved leaves allows them to drape comfortably against the square beads.

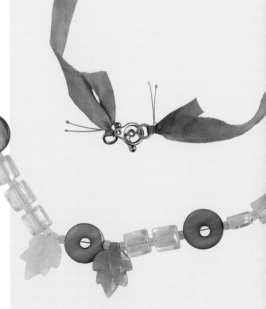

Asymmetrical necklace

Each side of this lovely necklace has a different distinctive look. The necklace fastens at the front by slipping cords knotted with a selection of pretty beads through a loop of freshwater pearls.

YOU WILL NEED

2 sterling silver crimp beads

45 cm (18 in) flexible beading wire

34 x 4 mm (⅙ in) silver baroque freshwater pearls

Wire snippers

Crimping pliers

31 x 8 mm (⁵⁄₁₆ in) dyed lilac jade beads

Silver gimp

No. 10 lilac carded bead cord

1 collapsible needle

3 x 1 cm (⅜ in) lilac donut ceramic beads

3 x 1 cm (⅜ in) lilac 'eye' glass lampwork beads

1 x 1.3 cm x 9 mm (½ x ⅜ in) lilac drop Bohemian rose lamp bead

3 x 5 cm (2 in) sterling silver ball pins

Snipe-nose pliers

Round-nose pliers

4 x 3 mm (⅛ in) sterling silver beads

2 x 4 cm (1½ in) long lilac handmade glass beads

Scissors

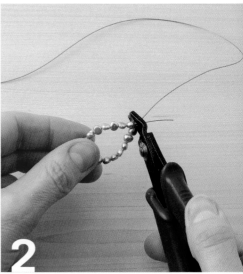

1 Thread a crimp bead then sixteen 4 mm (⅙ in) silver baroque freshwater pearls onto flexible beading wire. Insert 4 cm (1½ in) at one end of the beading wire through the crimp bead, making a loop of threaded pearls.

2 Secure the crimp bead using a pair of crimping pliers, referring to the **Using a crimp bead technique** on page 22. Snip off the excess beading wire with wire snippers.

TIP
The double threaded bead cord may be too thick to insert through some beads. In this case, thread the cords through separately. Alternatively, use a bead reamer to enlarge the holes.

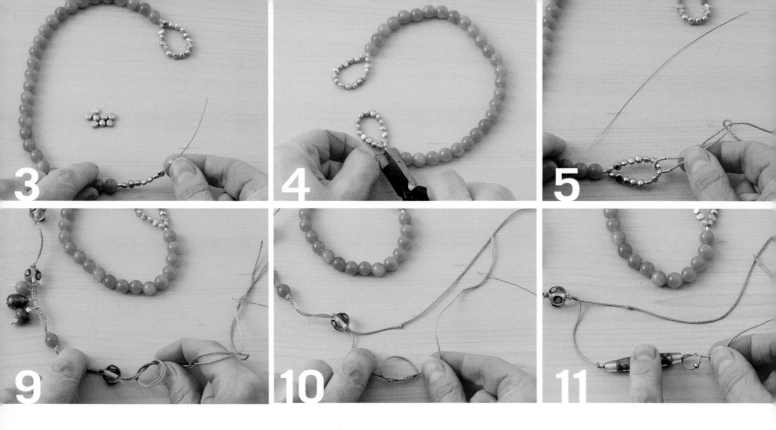

3 Thread twenty-eight 8 mm (⁵⁄₁₆ in) dyed lilac jade beads onto the beading wire. Slip on a crimp bead, then sixteen 4 mm (⅙ in) silver baroque freshwater pearls.

4 Insert the end of the beading wire through the crimp bead, making a loop of threaded pearls. Secure the crimp bead using a pair of crimping pliers as before. Snip off the excess beading wire with wire snippers.

5 Cut a 2 cm (¾ in) length of silver gimp with wire snippers. Slip the gimp onto the bead cord. Cut the cord to 130 cm (51 in) long. Slip the cord through one loop of pearls. Bend the cord in half, slip the

gimp along the cord to the centre. Thread both ends of cord onto a collapsible needle.

6 Thread on two 1 cm (⅜ in) lilac donut ceramic beads. Make a knot after the last bead. Make another knot 3.5 cm (1⅜ in) along the cords. Thread on a dyed lilac jade bead. Make a knot after the bead.

7 Make a knot 3.5 cm (1⅜ in) along the cords. Thread on a 1 cm (⅜ in) lilac 'eye' glass lampwork bead. Make a double knot after the bead. Repeat Step 7.

8 Refer to the **Making a wrapped loop technique** on page 19 to fix a a dyed lilac jade bead onto a ballpin using a pair

of snipe-nose and round-nose pliers. Fix a 1.3 cm x 9 mm (½ x ⅜ in) lilac drop Bohemian rose lamp bead onto a ballpin with a wrapped loop and a silver baroque freshwater pearl, a lilac donut bead and another silver baroque freshwater pearl onto another ballpin with a wrapped loop.

9 Slip the wrapped loops of the beads onto the cords. Make a double knot 3.5 cm (1⅜ in) from the last knot. Thread a dyed lilac jade bead onto the cords. Make a double knot after the bead. Make a double knot 3.5 cm (1⅜ in) from the last knot. Thread a lilac 'eye' glass lampwork bead onto both cords. Make a double knot after the bead.

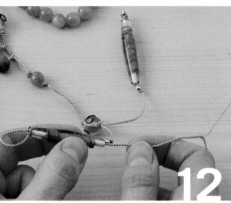

10 Pull one cord out of the needle to separate the cords. Make a knot on one cord 3.5 cm (1½ in) after the last knot and 5.5 cm (2¼ in) after the last knot on the other cord.

11 On one cord, thread on a 3 mm (⅛ in) sterling silver bead, a 4 cm (1½ in) long lilac handmade glass bead and silver bead. Tie the cord tightly around the cord between the long bead and last silver bead.

12 Insert the needle back through the long bead. Pull the thread and cut off the excess close to the top of the long bead with a pair of scissors. Repeat Steps 11 to 12 to finish the other cord.

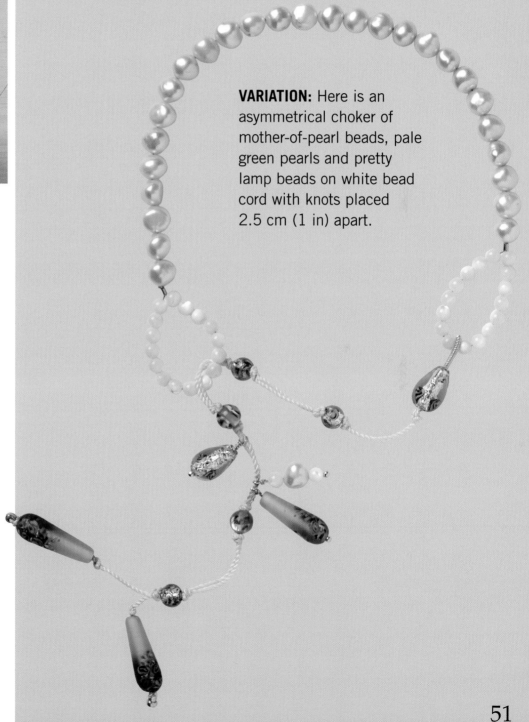

VARIATION: Here is an asymmetrical choker of mother-of-pearl beads, pale green pearls and pretty lamp beads on white bead cord with knots placed 2.5 cm (1 in) apart.

Two-strand necklace

A variety of beads in delicate shades of smokey grey combine to create this stunning necklace. The strings of fine beads are threaded through a beautiful tube bead of carved jade.

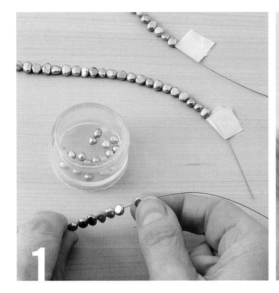

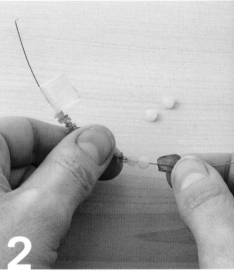

1 Snip two 60 cm (24 in) lengths of flexible beading wire with a pair of wire snippers. Tape 4 cm (1½ in) at one end of each beading wire with a piece of masking tape to stop the pearls slipping off. Thread pearls onto the beading wire for 31 cm (12¼ in). Tape the end of the beading wire with a piece of masking tape to stop the pearls slipping off. Repeat on the other beading wire.

2 Snip two 40 cm (16 in) lengths of beading wire with a pair of wire snippers. Tape 4 cm (1½ in) at one end of each beading wire with a piece of masking tape to stop the beads slipping off. Thread a sequence of labrodite chips for 3 cm (1¼ in), two 4 mm (⅙ in) jade disc beads, one labrodite facetted brick bead and two jade disc beads onto one length of beading wire.

3 Repeat the sequence adding more labrodite chips to match the threaded length of beads to the threaded lengths of pearls. Repeat on the other beading wire. Remove the end tapes on the pearls. Thread the four threaded beading wires through a 1 cm (⅜ in) diameter rutilated quartz bead.

4 Insert the beading wires through a crimp bead. Pull the beading wires tightly through the rutilated quartz bead and crimp. Secure the crimp bead using a pair of crimping pliers, referring to the **Using a crimp bead technique** on page 22.

5 Carefully snip off the two shorter beading wires with a pair of wire snippers below the crimp bead. Thread the two beading wires through a jade carved tube bead and a rutilated quartz bead.

6 Thread twelve pearls, one rutilated quartz bead, one crimp bead and one jade disc bead onto one beading wire. Insert the end of the beading wire back through the crimp bead.

7 Pull the beading wire tightly. Secure the crimp bead using a pair of crimping pliers, referring to the **Using a crimp bead technique** on page 22. Snip off the excess beading wire with wire snippers.

8 Thread labrodite chips for 2.5 cm (1 in), two 4 mm (⅙ in) jade disc beads, one labrodite facetted brick bead, two jade disc beads, labrodite chips for 2.5 cm (1 in), one rutilated quartz bead, one crimp bead and one jade disc bead onto the other beading wire.

9 Insert the end of the beading wire back through the crimp bead. Repeat Step 7 to secure the crimp bead in place.

10 Remove the masking tape at the start of the beading wires. Insert the beading wire of one string of pearls and beads through a crimp bead and the ring of a sterling silver necklace clasp. Insert the ends of the beading

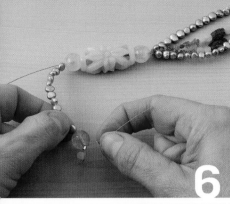

wire back through the crimp bead, suspending the necklace clasp.

11 Secure the crimp bead using a pair of crimping pliers, referring to the **Using a crimp bead technique** on page 22. Snip off the excess beading wire with wire snippers. Repeat on the other half of the necklace clasp.

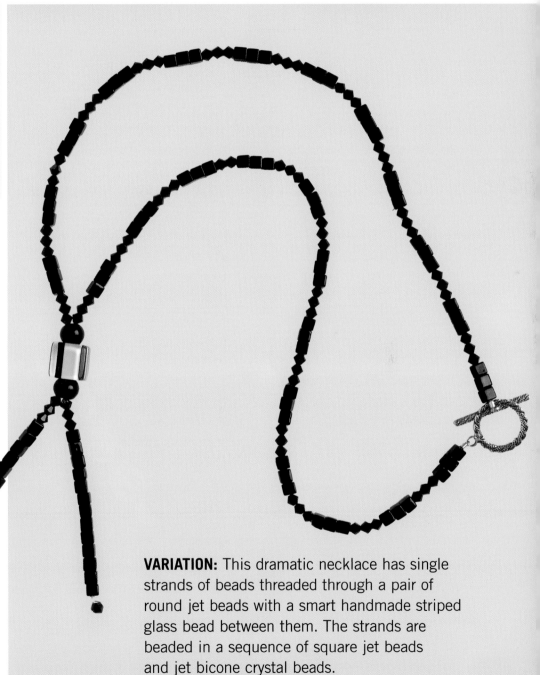

VARIATION: This dramatic necklace has single strands of beads threaded through a pair of round jet beads with a smart handmade striped glass bead between them. The strands are beaded in a sequence of square jet beads and jet bicone crystal beads.

55

Chunky stone necklace

Bold beads strung on silk cord are often knotted to stop them rubbing against each other. A knotted cord is used on this stunning necklace of rose quartz and rock crystal beads. A pair of brushed silver beads separate the three distinct sections of the necklace. The necklace is finished with gimp which will stop the clasp from rubbing against the cord.

YOU WILL NEED

2 m (2½ yd) of no. 5 pink carded bead cord

Collapsible needle

Approx. 24 graduated 1–1.5 cm (⅜–⅝ in) bati rose quartz beads

Large needle or awl

2 brushed sterling silver teardrop beads

Approx. 9 tumble rose quartz beads

Approx. 9 rock crystal broad bean beads

Silver gimp

Wire snippers

1 sterling silver stardust round necklace clasp

Scissors

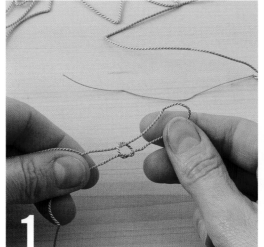

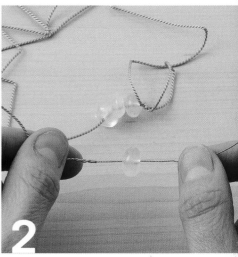

1 If the bead cord does not have a fixed needle, thread a 2 m (2¼ yd) length of pink bead cord onto a collapsible needle. Make a loose slip knot about 20 cm (8 in) from the end of the cord to stop the beads slipping off.

2 Starting with the smallest size, thread on the four smallest bati rose quartz beads in order of size. Slip the beads along the cord to the slip knot. The knots for the first four beads will be added later.

TIP
Gimp must be handled gently. Ideally, use the largest size gimp as it will uncoil if you try to thread a cord and needle through gimp that is too narrow.

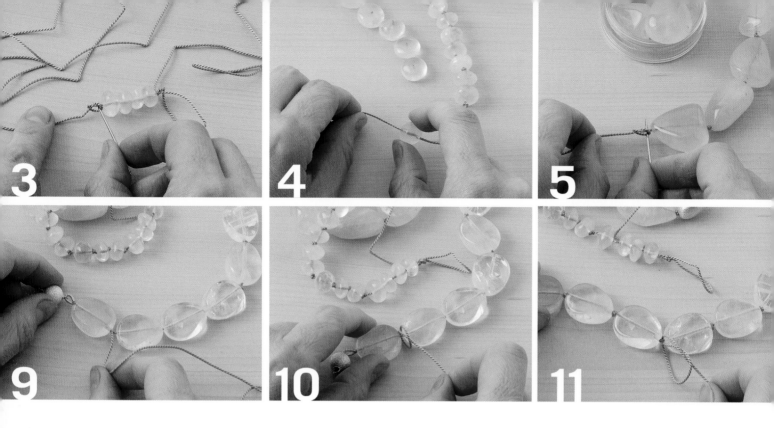

3 Make an overhand knot after the last bead, insert the point of a large needle into the loop of the knot and guide the knot along the cord to sit next to the bead. Pull the cord to tighten the knot. Make a double knot between all the beads if you prefer a distinctive looking knot.

4 Thread on the next bead and make a knot as before. The knots should be tight against the bead as the cord will stretch. Continue adding bati rose quartz beads, graduating the sizes and knotting the cord between the beads.

5 Make a knot after the last bead. Thread on a brushed sterling silver teardrop bead. Make a knot. Thread on nine tumble rose quartz beads, knotting the cord between the beads.

6 Make a knot after the last bead. Thread on a brushed sterling silver teardrop bead, facing the opposite direction to the first teardrop bead. Make a knot. Thread on five rock crystal broad bean beads, knotting the cord between the beads.

7 Make a knot after the last bead. Thread on four rock crystal broad bean beads.

8 Cut a 1 cm (⅜ in) length of silver gimp with wire snippers. Slip the gimp along the cord to the last bead. Insert the needle through the ring of the necklace clasp.

9 Insert the needle back through the last bead. Pull up the cord until there is a only a small space between the last two beads.

10 Knot the cord tightly around the threaded cord between the last two beads. Insert the needle through the second from last bead. Knot the cord tightly around the threaded cord between the second and third from last two beads.

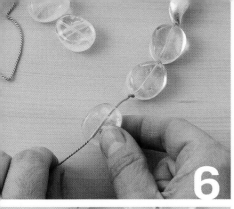

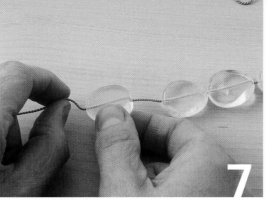

VARIATION: Here is a bold necklace of raw tumbled lapis beads strung on dark blue carded bead cord. Shiny rock crystal chips at each end of the necklace provide a stark contrast to the lapis beads.

11 Insert the needle through the third from last bead, knot the cord tightly around the threaded cord between the third and fourth from last two beads. Insert the needle through the fourth from last bead. Pull the cord taut and cut off the excess with a pair of scissors. The end of the cord will be neatly concealed in the fourth bead.

12 Remove the slip knot at the start of the necklace. Thread the cord onto a collapsible needle. Repeat Steps 8 to 11 to finish the other end of the necklace.

Wire leaf choker

This understated choker displays the pretty leaf pendant to great effect.
The pendant is simple to make from half hard sterling silver wire. Tiny turquoise
beads add a contrasting touch of colour to the vibrant pink cord.

YOU WILL NEED

11.5 cm (4½ in) of 18-gauge
 (1 mm) half hard sterling
 silver wire

Jewellery file

Snipe-nose pliers

Round-nose pliers

9 x 2 mm (¹⁄₁₂ in) turquoise bead

1 sterling silver eye pin

Wire snippers

50 cm (20 in) fine pink cotton cord

8 x 8 mm (⁵⁄₁₆ in) sterling silver
 teardrop beads

8 x 5 cm (2 in) sterling silver
 ballpins

Yanoacrylate glue

2 sterling silver cord ends

1 sterling silver bicone necklace
 clasp

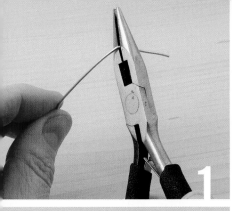

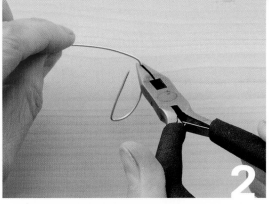

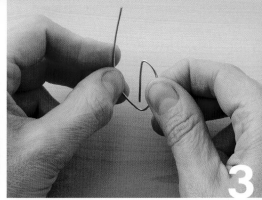

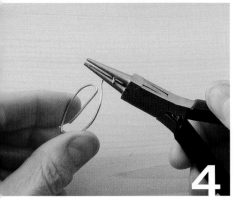

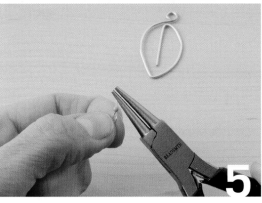

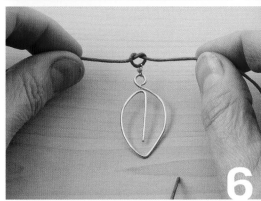

1 File the ends of the wire with a jewellery file to round the ends. Bend 2.5 cm (1 in) at one end at right angles to form the 'vein' of the leaf using a pair of snipe-nose pliers.

2 Bend the long end of the wire downwards in a curve between your fingers to form the side of the leaf. Bend the wire at a right angle 6 mm (¼ in) from the end of the vein using a pair of snipe nose pliers.

3 Bend the extending wire in a curve between your fingers towards the top of the leaf to form the opposite side of the leaf.

4 Hold the end of the wire with a pair of round-nose pliers. Coil the wire away from the leaf to form a loop.

5 Slip a 2 mm (¹⁄₁₂ in) turquoise bead onto an eye pin. Refer to the **Pinning beads technique** on page 20 to make a pinned bead. Open one eye and slip it onto the loop of the leaf.

6 Insert the fine pink cotton cord through the top eye of the pinned bead. Tie the pinned bead to the centre of the cord, suspending the leaf.

VARIATION: The wire leaves on this delightful pair of earrings are modelled from 7.5 cm (3 in) lengths of wire. The leaf 'veins' are 1.5 cm (⅝ in) long. The leaf hangs from pinned candy pink baroque freshwater pearl and 4 mm (⅙ in) light sapphire bicone crystal beads.

61

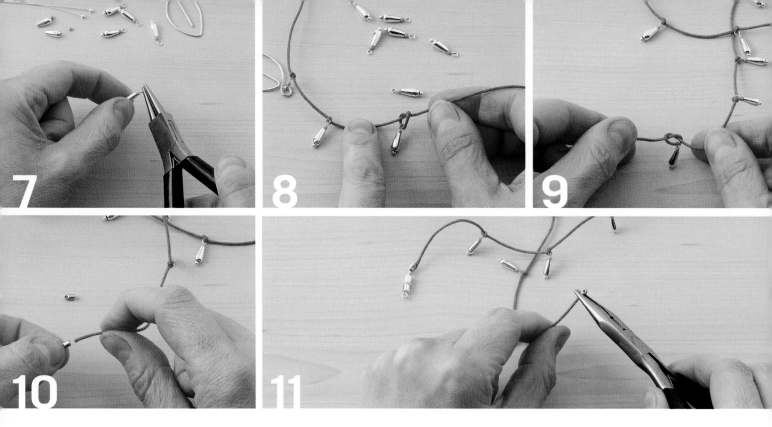

7 Slip an 8 mm ($^5/_{16}$ in) sterling silver teardrop bead and a 2 mm ($^1/_{12}$ in) turquoise bead onto a 5 cm (2 in) sterling silver ballpin. Refer to the **Making a single loop technique** on page 18 to fix the beads using a pair of snipe-nose and round-nose pliers. Repeat to fix beads on eight ballpins.

8 Slip the loop of one ballpin onto the cord. Tie the loop to the cord 2.5 cm (1 in) from the centre. Repeat to tie three ballpins onto the cord, tying them in place at 3.5 cm (1$^3/_8$ in) intervals.

9 Tie the loop of four ballpins in matching positions on the other end of the cord. With the leaf pendant centred, cut the cord 36 cm (14 in) long.

10 Dab one end of the cord with yanoacrylate glue and insert it into a cord end. Squeeze the cord end closed around the cord with a pair of snipe-nose pliers. Repeat at the other end of the cord.

11 Open the loop on a sterling silver bicone necklace clasp using two pairs of pliers. Slip the loop through the eye of one cord end. Close the loop with the pliers. Repeat at the other end of the choker.

Starburst brooch

Here is a pretty brooch of assorted semi-precious stone, crystal and pearl beads. The beads are fixed on twisted wires around a metal sieve that is covered with a mass of beads in lovely shades of sapphire and lilac. A brooch back is fixed behind the sieve.

YOU WILL NEED

3 m (3 1/3 yds) of 26-gauge (0.4 mm) sterling silver wire

Wire snippers

1 x 3 cm (1 1/4 in) silver coloured brooch back and sieve.

Snipe-nose pliers

Approx. 13 x 6 mm (1/4 in) tanzanite spacer crystal beads

Approx. 12 x 5 mm (1/4 in) violet facetted crystal beads

Approx. 12 x blue lace agate chips

Approx. 9 x 5 mm (1/4 in) violet opal bicone crystal bead

Approx. 14 x 6 x 4 mm (1/4 x 1/6 in) rectangular amethyst beads

Approx. 9 x 4 mm (1/6 in) magenta potato freshwater pearl beads

Approx. 9 x 4 mm (1/6 in) mauve potato freshwater pearl beads

3 x 8 mm (5/16 in) baby blue side drilled freshwater pearl beads

1 Snip a 60 cm (24 in) length of 26-gauge (0.4 mm) sterling silver wire using wire snippers. Insert 5 cm (2 in) at one end of the wire through a hole in the second from outer ring of holes on top of the sieve. Insert the short end of wire through a hole on the outer ring and 'sew' the wire between the two holes twice to secure in place, using a pair of snipe-nose pliers to pull the wire 'stitches' tight. Snip off the excess wire under the sieve.

2 Thread a 6 mm (¼ in) tanzanite spacer crystal bead onto the wire. Hold the bead 3 cm (1¼ in) from the outer edge of the sieve.

3 Cross the wire on itself under the bead then twist the wires together for 1.2 cm (½ in) under the bead.

4 Thread a 5 mm (¼ in) violet facetted crystal bead onto the wire. Hold the bead 1.2 cm (½ in) from the main wire. Cross the wire on itself under the bead then twist the wires together until you reach the main wire.

5 Twist the two wires together until you reach the edge of the sieve. Bring the wire to the right side through the next hole in the second from outer ring of holes.

6 Thread on a blue lace agate chip. Hold the bead 2.5 cm (1 in) from the outer edge of the sieve. Repeat Steps 2 to 5 to twist the wires and fix a mixture of tanzanite spacer crystal beads, violet facetted crystal beads, blue lace agate chips, rectangular amethyst beads, 5 mm (¼ in) violet opal bicone crystal beads, 4 mm (⅙ in) magenta freshwater pearls and 4 mm (⅙ in) mauve freshwater pearls, surrounding the sieve, having the outer beads or chips 3 cm (1¼ in) or 2.5 cm (1 in) from the edge of the sieve.

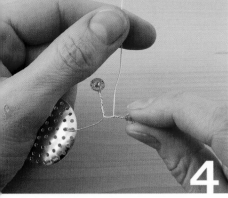

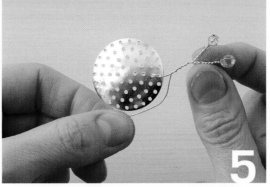

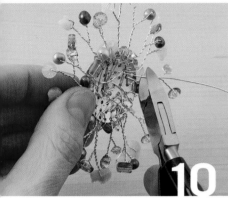

7 When you are close to running out of wire, sew the end of the wire twice between two holes in the sieve. Snip off the excess wire under the sieve. Repeat Step 1 to start the next length of wire and continue fixing wires and beads around the edge of the sieve.

8 Bring the wire to the right side through one of the outer holes. Thread on a magenta potato freshwater pearl bead. Take the wire to the underside of the sieve and thread it through to the front through the next hole along on the outer ring of holes and continue lacing beads and chips around the circumference of the sieve.

9 Bring the wire to the right side through an inner hole. Thread on an 8 mm (⁵⁄₁₆ in) baby blue side drilled freshwater pearl bead. Insert the wire through the next hole. Repeat to sew a mixture of beads and chips in the middle of the sieve.

10 To finish, sew the wire twice between two holes. Cut off the excess wire on the underside of the sieve.

11 Place the sieve on the brooch back. Squeeze the prongs of the brooch back over the edge of the sieve with a pair of snipe-nose pliers.

VARIATION: This pair of chunky clip-on earrings are made in the same way as the centre of the starburst brooch. Freshwater pearl, crystal and glass beads and semi-precious chips are sewn to a pair of small sieves that are fixed with snipe-nose pliers to clip-on earring backs.

Woven butterfly wing

A pair of sparkling butterfly shaped crystals are a beautiful feature on this ring woven with crystal beads and freshwater pearls. Pacific opal crystal beads co-ordinate well with the turquoise coloured pearls.

YOU WILL NEED

2 short beading needles

Fine bead cord

Approx. 11 x 5 mm (1/4 in) 'crystal' round facetted crystal beads

Approx. 11 turquoise baroque freshwater pearls

Approx. 11 x 5 mm (1/4 in) pacific opal round facetted crystal beads

12 x 3 mm (1/8 in) 'crystal' bicone crystal beads

2 crystal butterflies

Scissors

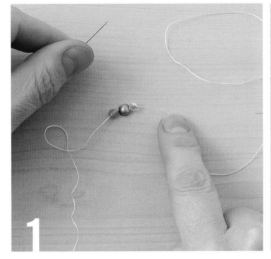

1 Thread a short beading needle with a 70 cm (28 in) length of fine bead cord. Thread on a 'crystal' round facetted crystal bead, a turquoise baroque freshwater pearl and a pacific opal round facetted crystal bead. Slide the round crystal beads and pearl to the centre of the bead cord.

2 Thread on a pearl. Thread the other end of the bead cord onto a second needle. Insert the second needle through the second pearl, towards the threaded beads and pearl. Pull the bead cords tight, forming a ring of round crystals beads and pearls.

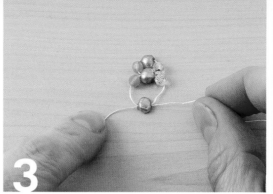

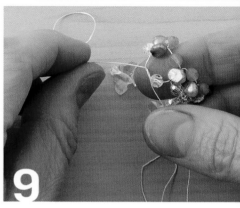

3 With the 'crystal' crystal bead on the right hand side, thread a 'crystal' crystal bead and a pearl onto the right hand bead cord and a pacific opal crystal bead onto the left hand bead cord. Insert the left hand needle through the last pearl.

4 Repeat Step 3 twice. Thread six 3 mm (⅛ in) 'crystal' bicone crystal beads onto the right hand bead cord. Insert the right hand needle down through one crystal butterfly and one 3 mm (⅛ in) 'crystal' bicone crystal bead.

5 Insert the needle back through the butterfly and the first six bicone crystals. Pull the bead cord to suspend the butterfly.

6 Repeat Step 3. Thread four bicone crystal beads, one crystal butterfly and one bicone crystal bead onto the right hand bead cord. Insert the needle back through the butterfly and first four bicone crystal beads. Pull the bead cord to suspend the butterfly. Repeat Step 3 four times.

TIP
Baroque pearls often have very small holes. Use a small size beading needle such as size 12 to thread the beads.

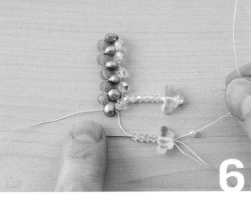

VARIATION: The bicone crystal beads and butterflies have been omitted from this lovely woven ring of black diamond crystal beads and coral baroque pearls.

7 Thread a pacific opal crystal bead onto the left hand bead cord. Thread a 'crystal' round crystal bead onto the right hand bead cord.

8 Insert the left hand bead cord through the first pearl. Pull the bead cords tight to form the ring.

9 Check the size of the ring. If you would like to enlarge it, slip the bead cord out of the first pearl and repeat Steps 3, 7 and 8. Knot the bead cords together in a double knot.

10 Weave the bead cords through the crystal beads and pearls. Cut off the excess bead cord with a pair of scissors.

Chain and bead necklace

A chain necklace is always popular and a few added beads will make it extra special. The soft colours of the chalcedony and florite beads used here blend together perfectly.

1 Refer to the **Pinning beads technique** on page 20 to fix four 4 mm (⅙ in) pacific opal round facetted crystal beads, two 1 cm (⅜ in) chalcedony tumble beads and five 1 cm (⅜ in) florite tumble beads onto 26-gauge (0.4 mm) gold-filled wire using a pair of snipe-nose and round-nose pliers.

2 Snip a 14.5 cm (5⅝ in) length of 2.5 mm (⅛ in) wide gold-filled chain with wire snippers. Open one loop of a pinned pacific opal crystal bead. Slip one end of the chain onto the loop. Close the loop using two pairs of pliers.

TIP
Use the tip of a cocktail stick to dab a little clear nail varnish on the joins of jump rings to secure them.

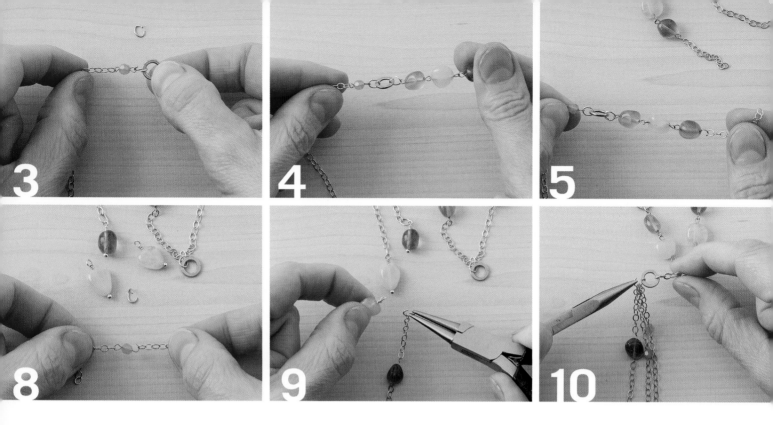

3 Open two 7 x 5 mm ($\frac{5}{32}$ x $\frac{1}{4}$ in) gold-filled oval jump rings. Slip the other loop of the pinned pacific opal bead and one 8 mm ($\frac{5}{16}$ in) vermeil closed ring onto one jump ring. Close the jump ring.

4 Link a pinned chalcedony tumble bead between two pinned florite tumble beads referring to the **Pinning beads technique** on page 20. Slip the vermeil closed ring and the top loop of the linked chalcedony and florite beads onto the other jump ring. Close the jump ring.

5 Snip a 3 cm (1$\frac{1}{4}$ in) length of chain with wire snippers. Open the lower loop of the linked chalcedony and florite beads. Slip one end of the chain onto the loop. Close the loop. Repeat Steps 2 to 5 to make the other side of the necklace.

6 Open another jump ring. Slip both ends of the short chain and a vermeil closed ring onto the jump ring. Close the jump ring.

7 Snip a 1.5 cm ($\frac{5}{8}$ in) and a 3 cm (1$\frac{1}{4}$ in) length of chain with wire snippers. Fix a pinned pacific opal crystal bead between the lengths of chain. Refer to the **Making a wrapped loop technique** on page 19 to fix a florite tumble bead and two chalcedony tumble

beads onto ballpins. Open a jump ring. Slip the end of the longer chain and the wrapped florite bead onto the jump ring. Close the jump ring.

8 Snip two 3 cm (1$\frac{1}{4}$ in) lengths of chain with wire snippers. Fix a pinned pacific opal crystal bead between the lengths of chain. Open a jump ring. Slip one end of the chain and a chalcedony wrapped bead onto the jump ring. Close the jump ring.

9 Snip two 2 cm ($\frac{3}{4}$ in) lengths of chain with wire snippers. Fix a pinned florite bead between the lengths of chain. Open a jump ring. Slip one end of the chain and a wrapped chalcedony bead onto the jump ring. Close the jump ring.

VARIATION: This sterling silver chain has pinned 5 mm (¼ in) coral pink glass and peach freshwater pearls anchored with a hammered sterling silver closed oval ring.

10 Open a jump ring. Slip the lower vermeil closed ring and the top of the three 'hanging' chains onto the jump ring. Close the jump ring.

11 Open a jump ring. Slip the end of the chain on one side of the necklace and the snake of a necklace clasp onto the jump ring. Close the jump ring. Repeat to fix the ring of the necklace clasp to the other end of the necklace.

Chain drop earrings

The five-hole end bars used to suspend sparkling crystal beads on these dramatic earrings are usually associated with multi-strand necklaces and bracelets but they are also great for hanging beads on earrings. Short lengths of chain suspend more crystal and pearl beads to create an elaborate chandelier style.

YOU WILL NEED

8 x 6 mm (¼ in) dark aqua spacer crystal beads

10 gold-filled eyepins

2 x gold-filled five-hole end bars

Round-nose pliers

Snipe-nose pliers

2 x tanzanite facetted crystal drop beads

3 cm (1¼ in) of 26-gauge (0.4 mm) gold-filled wire

Wire snippers

6 x 4 mm (⅙ in) siam bicone crystal beads

4 x 7 x 5 mm (5⁄32 x ¼ in) gold-filled oval jump rings

6 x 4 mm (⅙ in) light sapphire bicone crystal beads

4 x 3.5 cm (1⅜ in) gold-filled ballpins

8 x 3 x 5 mm (⅛ x ¼ in) white rondel freshwater pearls

10 cm (4 in) of 2.5 mm (⅛ in) wide gold-filled chain

4 x 4 mm (⅙ in) amethyst bicone crystal beads

2 x 1 cm (⅜ in) siam crystal hearts

Pair of gold-filled fish hook earring wires

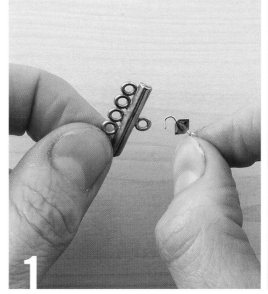

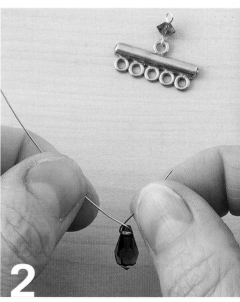

1 Refer to the **Pinning beads technique** on page 20 to fix a 6 mm (¼ in) dark aqua spacer crystal bead onto a gold-filled eyepin. Open one loop of the pinned bead and slip it onto the top ring of a gold-filled five-hole end bar. Close the loop using round-nose and snipe-nose pliers.

2 Slip a tanzanite facetted crystal drop bead onto an 8 cm (3⅛ in) length of 26-gauge (0.4 mm) gold-filled wire with 2 cm (¾ in) of the wire extending at one side. Pull the wires tightly across the top of the bead.

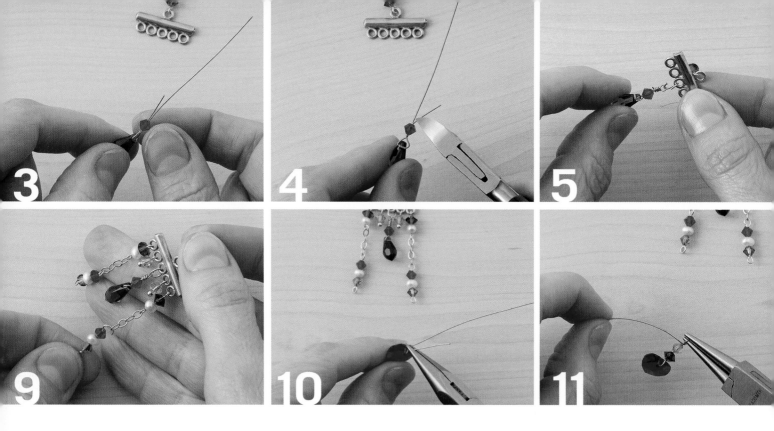

3 Use a pair of snipe-nose pliers to bend each wire upwards at the point where the two wires cross. Thread a 4 mm (⅙ in) siam bicone crystal bead onto both wires.

4 Snip the short end of wire 3 mm (⅛ in) above the top of the siam bead with wire snippers. Refer to Steps 3 to 6 of **Wrapping a side or top drilled bead technique** on page 21 to finish wrapping the beads.

5 Open a 7 x 5 mm (⁵⁄₃₂ x ¼ in) gold-filled oval jump ring. Slip the loop of the wrapped beads and the centre ring of the five-hole end bar onto the jump ring. Close the jump ring using two pairs of pliers.

6 Refer to the **Making a single loop technique** on page 18 to fix two 4 mm (⅙ in) light sapphire bicone crystal beads onto 3.5 cm (1⅜ in) gold-filled ballpins. Open the loops and hang on the second and forth rings of the end bar.

7 Refer to the **Pinning beads technique** on page 20 to fix a dark aqua spacer crystal bead and a 3 x 5 mm (⅛ x ¼ in) white rondel freshwater pearl onto an eyepin. Repeat to make another pinned bead. Open the loop above the dark aqua crystal beads and slip them onto the first and last ring in the five-hole end bar. Close the loops using two pairs of pliers.

8 Open the loops under the pearl beads. Snip two 1.2 cm (½ in) lengths of 2.5 mm (⅛ in) wide gold-filled chain with wire snippers. Hang one end of the chains onto the loops. Close the loops using two pairs of pliers.

9 Refer to the **Pinning beads technique** on page 20 to fix a siam bicone crystal bead, a white rondel freshwater pearl and a 4 mm (⅙ in) amethyst bicone crystal bead onto an eye pin. Repeat to make another pinned bead. Open the loop above the siam beads and hook onto the end of the chains. Close the loops.

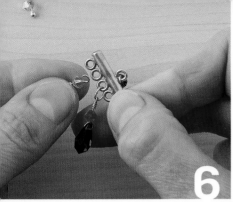

VARIATION: Here is an elegant pair of chain drop earrings. Wrapped turquoise and crystal hearts and 4 mm (⅙ in) back diamond bicone crystal beads hang on jump rings from 4 cm (1½ in) and 2.5 cm (1 in) lengths of chain.

10 Slip a 1 cm (⅜ in) siam crystal heart onto an 8 cm (3⅛ in) length of wire with 2 cm (¾ in) of the wire extending at one side. Pull the wires tightly across the top of the heart. Use a pair of snipe-nose pliers to bend each wire upwards at the point where the two wires cross. Thread a dark aqua spacer crystal bead and a light sapphire bicone crystal bead onto both wires.

11 Snip the short end of wire 3 mm (⅛ in) above the top of the siam bead with wire snippers. Refer to Steps 3 to 6 of **Wrapping a side or top drilled bead technique** on page 21 to finish wrapping the beads. Open the loops under the pinned amethyst beads. Hook the loop at the top of the wrapped beads

onto the loops of the pinned beads. Close the loops.

12 Open a jump ring. Slip the eye of a gold-filled fish hook earring wire and the loop of the pinned dark aqua bead onto the jump ring. Close the jump ring using two pairs of pliers. Make a matching earring.

Three-strand choker

This dramatic choker of stunning crystals is just the thing for a glamourous event. Three rows of crystal beads in co-ordinating colours are secured through three-hole spacer bars and hung with beautiful facetted crystal hearts.

YOU WILL NEED

2 x 4 mm (⅛ in) sterling silver jump rings

1 sterling silver necklace clasp

2 sterling silver three-hole end bars

4 sterling silver three-hole spacer bars

175 cm (70 in) flexible beading wire

Wire snippers

Masking tape

Approx. 80 x 4 mm (⅛ in) light sapphire bicone crystal beads

Approx. 80 x 4 mm (⅛ in) sapphire bicone crystal beads

Approx. 160 x 4 mm (⅛ in) amethyst AB2 bicone crystal beads

60 cm (24 in) of 26-gauge (0.4 mm) sterling silver wire

4 x 1 cm (⅜ in) sapphire crystal hearts

2 x 1.7 cm (1¹⁄₁₆ in) amethyst AB2 crystal hearts

2 x 1 cm (⅜ in) light sapphire crystal hearts

Snipe-nose pliers

Round-nose pliers

8 sterling silver crimp beads

Crimping pliers

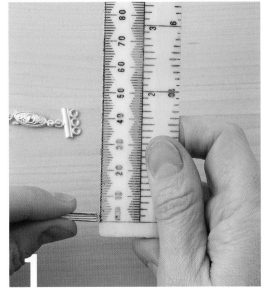

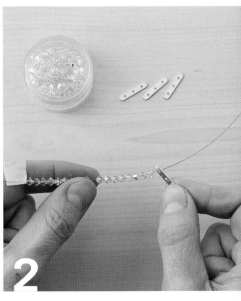

1 Decide upon the finished length you wish the choker to be. Fix jump rings to the necklace clasp then to the end bars. Measure the width of the end bars with the jump rings and clasp between them. Measure the depth of the four spacer bars. Take both these measurements off the finished choker length. Divide this final measurement by five.

2 Snip three 45 cm (18 in) lengths of flexible beading wire using wire snippers. Wrap a piece of masking tape 7.5 cm (3 in) from one end of each length to stop the beads slipping off. Thread 4 mm (⅛ in) light sapphire bicone crystal beads for the 'one fifth' measurement onto one tiger tail. You will need an even number of beads for each five sections of the choker. If necessary, thread on less beads rather than more to achieve an even number. Thread the beading wire through the top hole of a spacer bar.

3 Continue threading on light sapphire bicone crystal beads until you have five equal sections of beads with spacer bars between them. Wrap a piece of masking tape around the beading wire after the last bead.

4 On the second length of beading wire, repeat to thread on 4 mm (⅙ in) sapphire bicone crystal beads in the same way, but threading the beading wire through the centre hole of the spacer bars.

5 Thread the required number of 4 mm (⅙ in) amethyst AB2 bicone crystal beads onto the third beading wire. Insert the beading wire through the lower hole of the first spacer bar. Thread on half the

required number of bicone beads for the next section. Refer to the **Wrapping a side or top drilled bead technique** on page 21 to make on loop on the heart crystal beads using 0.4 mm thick sterling silver wire.

6 Thread a sapphire crystal heart onto the beading wire then half the required number of bicone beads. Insert the beading wire through the lower hole of the second spacer bar. Thread on half the required number of bicone beads for the next section. Thread on a 1.7 cm (1¹⁄₁₆ in) amethyst AB2 crystal heart. Finish the second half of the third row to match the first half.

7 Snip a 40 cm (16 in) length of beading wire.

Insert one end through a crimp bead and the lower hole of the first spacer bar. Insert 4 cm (1¾ in) of the beading wire back through the crimp bead, pull the beading wire tight but allow some movement. Secure the crimp bead using a pair of crimping pliers, referring to the **Using a crimp bead technique** on page 22. Snip off the excess beading wire with wire snippers.

8 Thread on thirteen amethyst AB2 bicone crystal beads, one light sapphire crystal heart and eleven amethyst AB2 bicone crystal beads. Insert the beading wire through the lower hole of the second spacer bar and down through the last bicone bead. Pull the beading wire tight.

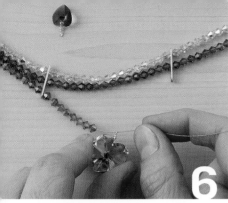

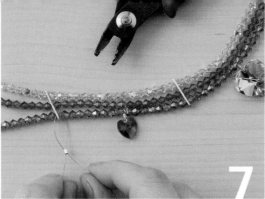

VARIATION: This pretty bracelet has two three-hole spacer bars between three strands of beautiful freshwater pearls in natural colours. When working out the length of the strands, divide the final measurement by three instead of five as described in Step 1.

9 Thread on ten amethyst AB2 bicone crystal beads, one sapphire crystal heart, four black diamond AB bicone crystal beads, one black diamond AB crystal heart, four black diamond AB bicone crystal beads, one sapphire crystal heart and eleven amethyst AB2 bicone crystal beads. Insert the beading wire through the lower hole of the third spacer bar and down through the last bicone bead. Pull the beading wire tight.

10 Thread on ten amethyst AB2 bicone crystal beads, one light sapphire crystal heart, thirteen amethyst AB2 bicone crystal beads and a crimp bead. Insert the beading wire through the lower hole of the fourth spacer bar and down

through the crimp bead. Secure the crimp bead using a pair of crimping pliers. Snip off the excess tiger beading wire with wire snippers.

11 Remove the masking tape. Check the length of the choker, allowing space for the end bars, jump rings and necklace clasp. Add more beads at each end if needed. Insert one end of the top beading wire through a crimp bead and the top ring of one end bar. Insert the end of the beading wire back through the crimp bead, suspending the end bars and necklace fastening.

12 Secure the crimp bead using a pair of crimping pliers. Snip off the excess beading wire with wire snippers. Repeat on the second and third beading wire. Push the beads and spacer bars along the beading wires. Fix the other end of the beading wires to the other end bar with crimp beads as before.

Multi-strand bracelet

This elaborate bracelet has five strands of assorted semi-precious beads in soft, co-ordinating colours. The strands are anchored through five-hole spacer bars and neatened with end caps.

YOU WILL NEED

2 sterling silver eye pins

2 x 4 mm (⅙ in) jump rings

Snipe-nose pliers

Round-nose pliers

1 sterling silver star and bar necklace clasp

Pair of 1 cm (⅜ in) sterling silver end caps

12 x purple square cat's eye beads

Wire snippers

140 cm (55 in) flexible beading wire

Masking tape

2 five-hole sterling silver spacer bars

30 x 6 x 4 mm (¼ x ⅙ in) rectangular amethyst beads

10 x 8 mm (⁵⁄₁₆ in) pacific opal facetted rondels

1 string of apatite chips

10 x 3 mm (⅛ in) sterling silver beads

10 x 1 cm (⅜ in) florite tumble beads

10 x amethyst chips

5 x 1 cm (⅜ in) chalcedony tumble beads

10 x 1 mm (¹⁄₁₆ in) crimp beads

Crimping pliers

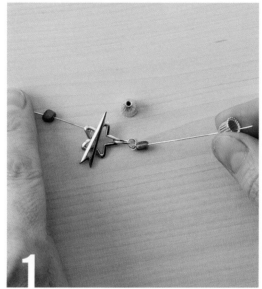

1 To calculate the length of the bracelet, slip the eye of each eye pin onto a 4 mm (⅙ in) jump ring. Fix the jump rings onto the ring at each side of a star and bar necklace clasp using a pair of snipe-nose and round-nose pliers. Fasten the necklace clasp. Thread one purple square cat's eye bead and an end cap onto each eye pin.

2 Lay the piece flat and measure the length. Subtract the desired bracelet length from the first measurement. Use wire snippers to snip five lengths of flexible beading wire 10 cm (4 in) longer than the final measurement. Remove the eye pins and set the cat's eye beads and end caps aside.

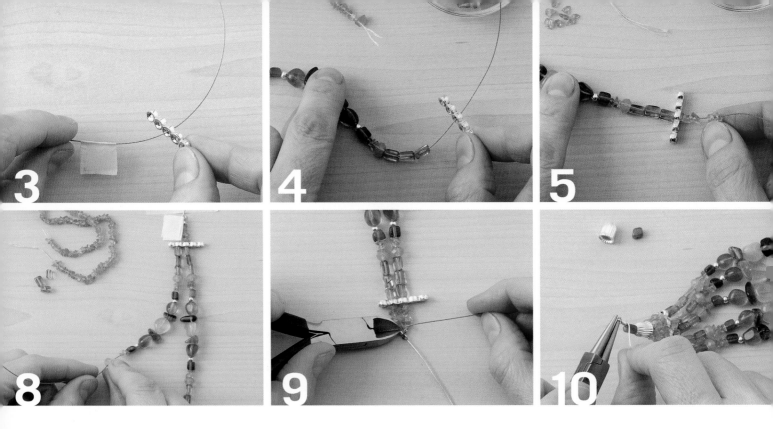

3 Wrap a piece of masking tape around one end of each beading wire 4 cm (1½ in) from one end to stop the beads slipping off. Insert the first beading wire through the centre hole of a five-hole sterling silver spacer bar.

4 Thread on three 6 x 4 mm (¼ x ⅙ in) rectangular amethyst beads, one 8 mm (⁵⁄₁₆ in) pacific opal facetted rondel, apatite chips for 5 mm (¼ in), one purple square cat's eye bead, one 3 mm (⅛ in) sterling silver bead, one 1 cm (⅜ in) florite tumble bead, one amethyst chip and one 1 cm (⅜ in) 1 cm (⅜ in) chalcedony tumble bead. The 1 cm (⅜ in) chalcedony tumble bead will be the centre of the bracelet. Bead the other half of the beading wire to match the first

half. Thread the beading wire through the centre hole of the other spacer bar.

5 Remove the masking tape. Thread equal amounts of apatite chips at each end of the beading wire until the beaded beading wire is the required measurement. Tape one end of the beading wire to stop the beads slipping off.

6 Thread on a crimp bead and eye pin. Insert the beading wire back through the crimp bead, leave a small loop of beading wire through the eye pin that allows for some movement.

7 Refer to the **Using a crimp bead technique** on page 22 to fix the crimp bead in place using a pair of crimping pliers. Snip off the excess beading wire with wire snippers. Push the beads and chips along the beading wire to the eyepin. Remove the tape and repeat to fix the other end to an eye pin with a crimp bead.

8 Tape one eye pin to your work surface to hold the bracelet steady. At the taped end, insert a beading wire through the next hole on the spacer bar. Repeat Step 4, checking that the centre bead and spacer bars are parallel, add more apatite chips to keep the beads level if necessary.

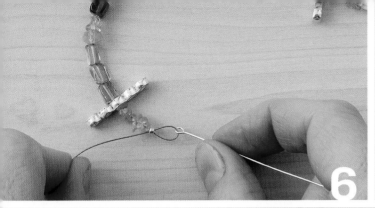

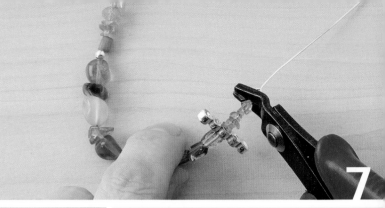

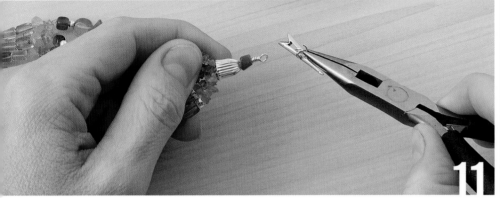

VARIATION: Lovely shades of pink combine on this multi-stranded bracelet of pearls, glass foil lined beads, rock crystal chips, rose quartz chips, opaque glass beads and tourmaline chips.

9 Remove the tape at the start of the beading wire. Thread on apatite chips. You will need more apatite chips than on the first beading wire to allow for the outer strand leaning in to meet the eye pin, thread on more apatite chips as required. Thread on a crimp bead. Insert the beading wire through the eye of the eye pin then back through the crimp bead, leave a small loop of beading wire through the eye pin that allows for some movement. Fix the crimp bead in place as before with a pair of crimping pliers. Repeat at the other end of the beading wire.

10 Working outwards from the centre, bead and fix the other beading wires between the eye pins. Thread an end cap onto one eye pin. It will cover the crimped ends of the beading wire. Thread on one purple square cat's eye bead. Refer to the **Making a wrapped loop technique** on page 19 to make a wrapped loop above the bead. Repeat on the other end of the bracelet.

11 Use a pair of snipe-nose and round-nose pliers to open a jump ring on the necklace clasp. Slip the loop of one wrapped loop onto the jump ring. Close the jump ring using the pliers. Repeat at the other end of the bracelet.

Tied flower lariat

At about 90cm (one yard) long, this charming lariat can be worn in a variety of ways. Subtlely coloured velvet flowers are interspersed along the lariat amongst beads and pearls of toning colours.

YOU WILL NEED

43 assorted crystal, glass, freshwater pearl and jade beads ranging from 5 mm (¼ in) to 2 cm (¾ in) diameter in shades of amber, green, light blue and grey

Approx. 41 x 3.5 cm (1⅜ in) gold-filled ballpins

Approx. 7 x 5 cm (2 in) gold-filled ballpins

Snipe-nose pliers

Round-nose pliers

8 x 2 cm (¾ in) diameter pale blue and fawn velvet flowers

4 x 5 mm (¼ in) black diamond round facetted crystal beads

14 x 8 mm (⁵⁄₁₆ in) sterling silver jump rings

Wire snippers

Light blue no.12 carded bead cord

Yanoacrylate glue

Scissors

TIP

When tying jump rings and loops of the flowers to the bead cord, position the flowers towards the ends of the bead cord.

1 Slip the assorted crystal, freshwater pearl, glass and jade beads onto ballpins; use 3.5 cm (1⅜ in) ballpins for the smaller beads and 5 cm (2 in) ballpins for larger or longer beads. If the glass beads have large holes, thread on a crystal bead first. Refer to the **Making a wrapped loop technique** on page 19 to fix the beads using a pair of snipe-nose and round-nose pliers.

2 Carefully pull or cut the flower heads off their stems and remove the stamens. Slip a 5 mm (¼ in) black diamond round facetted crystal bead onto four 3.5 cm (1⅜ in) ballpins. With wrong sides facing, thread two flowers onto each ballpin.

3 Snip the wire 1 cm (⅜ in) above the last flower using wire snippers. Hold the end of the ballpin with a pair of round-nose pliers 3 mm (⅛ in) from the tip of the jaws. Bend the wire towards you to make a loop that is centred over the flower. Repeat on all the ballpins.

4 Set one large bead aside. Open the jump rings using two pairs of pliers. Slip the wrapped loops of two large beads or three small beads onto each jump ring. Close the jump rings using two pairs of pliers.

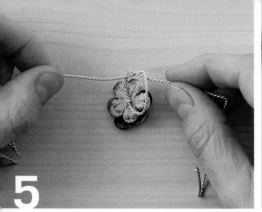

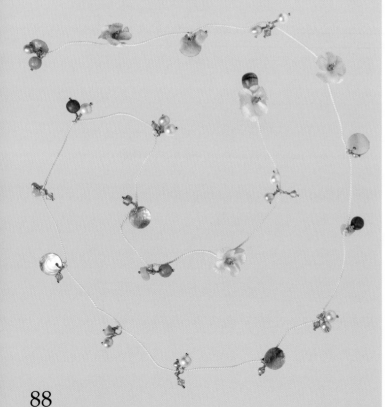

VARIATION: Here is a delicately coloured lariat of cream flowers, pale green and cream pearls, violet crystal beads, amethyst beads, blue lace agate chips and mother-of-pearl discs.

5 Slip the loop of one flower onto a 135 cm (53 in) length of light blue no. 12 bead cord. Tie the loop to the cord 15 cm (6 in) from one end.

6 Set one jump ring and one flower aside. Slip the other jump rings and loops of the flowers onto the cord, tying them in place at 5 cm (2 in) intervals.

7 Slip the set aside flower and large bead onto the bead cord and tie them to the cord with a double knot 5 cm (2 in) after the last jump ring.

8 Slip the set aside jump ring of beads onto the other end of the bead cord and tie them to the cord with a double knot 5 cm (2 in) after the flower.

9 Dab the end knots with glue and leave to dry. Cut off the excess cord close to the end knots with a pair of scissors.

Ladder bracelet

Simple bead weaving is used to make this beautiful bracelet. A fabulous ladder effect is achieved by using long drilled freshwater pearl beads bordered with button top drilled pearls.

YOU WILL NEED

6 mm (¼ in) round sterling silver stardust necklace clasp

2 x 5 mm (¼ in) sterling silver jump rings

2 sterling silver calotte crimps

Round-nose pliers

Snipe-nose pliers

Fine bead cord

Scissors

Masking tape

2 long beading needles

Approx. 52 lilac button top drilled freshwater pearl beads

Approx. 20 peacock long drilled freshwater pearl beads

Cyanoacrylate adhesive

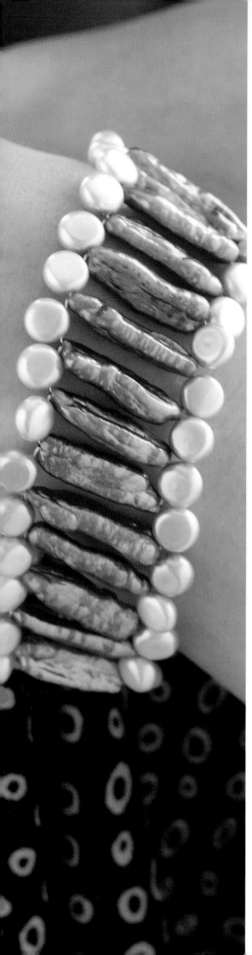

1 To calculate the length of the bracelet, slip a jump ring onto each end of the necklace clasp. Slip a calotte crimp onto each jump ring. Close the jump ring using a pair of round-nose and snipe-nose pliers. Lay the piece out flat and measure the length. For the final measurement, subtract this measurement plus 3 cm (1¼ in) from the desired bracelet length. Remove the calotte crimps.

2 Cut two 120 cm (48 in) lengths of fine bead cord. Wrap a piece of masking tape around the bead cords 15 cm (6 in) from one end to stop the beads slipping off. Thread a long beading needle onto each bead cord. Thread three lilac button top drilled freshwater pearl beads onto each bead cord.

3 Thread a peacock long drilled freshwater pearl bead onto one bead cord. Insert the other bead cord through the long drilled bead in the other direction.

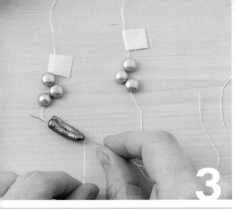

3

4

5

8

9

VARIATION: This copper coloured bracelet has long drilled freshwater pearls graduated in size so the longest beads are concentrated at the centre. The bracelet is bordered with baroque freshwater pearls and fastens with gold-filled findings.

4 Thread a button bead onto each bead cord, keeping the top drilled edge of the bead towards the long drilled bead.

5 Repeat Steps 3 and 4 until the bracelet measures the final measurement described in Step 1 between the centres of the first and last long drilled beads.

6 Thread two lilac button top drilled freshwater pearl beads onto each bead cord. Insert both bead cords through the hole in a calotte crimp.

7 Remove the masking tape at the start of the bracelet and insert both bead cords through the hole in a calotte crimp. Tie the bead cords securely together in a double knot over the hole of the calotte crimp. Cut off the excess bead cord close to the knots.

8 Dab cyanoacrylate adhesive on the knots to secure them in place. Close the cups of the calotte crimps with a pair of snipe-nose pliers.

9 Slip a calotte crimp onto each jump ring on the necklace clasp. Close the jump rings using two pairs of pliers.

91

Twisted necklace

If you have a feature pendant, this necklace is a great way of showing it off. Twist the necklace a few times before you wear it, the tighter the strings of beads are twisted, the shorter the necklace will be. The necklace fastens with an extension chain so the length can be further adjusted.

YOU WILL NEED

180 cm (72 in) flexible beading wire

Masking tape

28 x 3 mm (⅛ in) round hematite beads

26 x 1.2 cm (½ in) hematite cylindrical beads

7 x sterling silver crimp beads

2 sterling silver eye pins

Crimping pliers

Wire snippers

Approx. 114 x 4 mm (⅛ in) light green pressed glass beads

Approx. 69 x 6 mm (¼ in) round rock crystal beads

Pair of 1 cm (⅜ in) Bali style sterling silver end caps

4 x 4 mm (⅛ in) sterling silver jump rings

Snipe-nose pliers

Round-nose pliers

Sterling silver lobster claw necklace clasp

1 x 3.5 cm (1⅜ in) sterling silver ballpin

Sterling silver extension chain

Handmade glass pendant

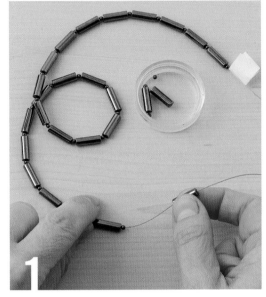

1 Wrap a piece of masking tape around the end of a 55 cm (25 in) length of flexible beading wire to stop the beads slipping off. Thread a sequence of a 3 mm (⅛ in) round hematite bead and a 1.2 cm (½ in) hematite cylindrical bead twenty-six times onto the beading wire. Thread on another 3 mm (⅛ in) round hematite bead.

2 Insert the end of the beading wire through a crimp bead and the eye of an eye pin. Insert the beading wire back through the crimp bead and pull the end of the flexible beading wire to tighten the loop of the beading wire through the eye pin.

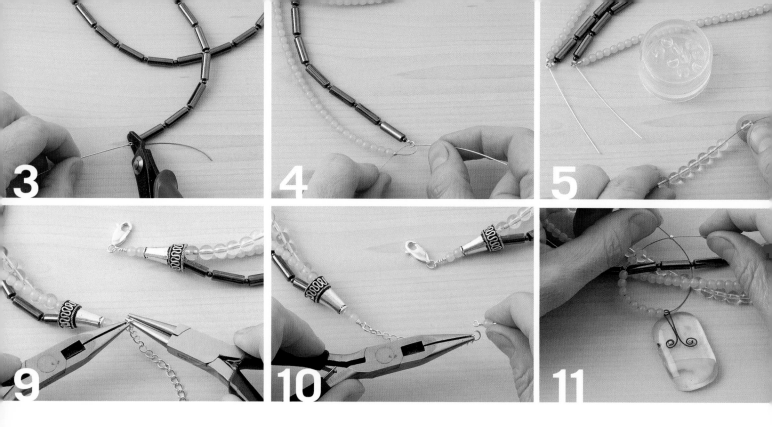

3 Refer to the **Using a crimp bead technique** on page 22 to fix the crimp bead with a pair of crimping pliers. Snip off the excess beading wire with a pair of wire snippers. Repeat at the other end of the beading wire.

4 Thread 4 mm (⅙ in) light green pressed glass beads onto beading wire until the beads are the same length as the hematite beads. Fix the beaded beading wire to the eye pins with crimp beads as before.

TIP
A twisted necklace also looks great without a pendant.

5 Thread 6 mm (¼ in) round rock crystal beads onto beading wire until the beads are the same length as the hematite beads. Fix the beaded beading wire to the eye pins with crimp beads as before.

6 Insert one eye pin through an end cap and two green pressed glass beads. Refer to the **Making a wrapped loop technique** on page 19 to make a wrapped loop above the last bead. Repeat at the other end of the necklace.

7 Open a 4 mm (⅙ in) sterling silver jump ring. Slip a lobster claw necklace clasp and the loop of the wrapped loop onto the jump ring. Close the jump ring using a pair of snipe-nose and round-nose pliers.

8 Slip a green pressed glass bead onto a 3.5 cm (1⅜ in) sterling silver ballpin. Refer to the **Making a wrapped loop technique** on page 19 to make a wrapped loop above the bead.

9 Open a jump ring. Slip the loop of the wrapped bead and one end of the extension chain onto the ring. Close the ring using two pairs of pliers.

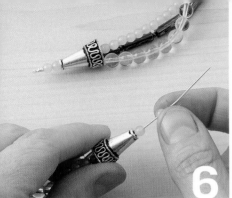

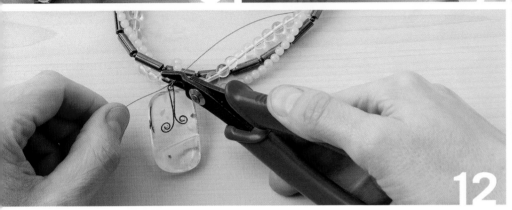

VARIATION: Two strings of turquoise chips and one of delicate apatite chips are twisted together and suspend a fabulous tourmalinated green quartz heart pendant.

10 Open another jump ring. Slip the loop of the wrapped bead and end of the chain onto the jump ring. Close the ring using two pairs of pliers.

11 Thread a handmade glass pendant facing forward, ten green pressed glass beads and a crimp bead onto a 13 cm (5¼ in) length of beading wire. Wrap the beading wire around the necklace and insert the other end through the crimp bead.

12 Pull the beading wire tight and fix the crimp bead with a pair of crimping pliers. Snip off the excess beading wire.

Rosette brooch

The glorious flower effect of this stunning brooch is achieved by sewing petal shaped or drop beads in diminishing circles to a metal sieve. The beads used must be side drilled across one end so they can be sewn with fine wire.

YOU WILL NEED

Approx. 120 cm (48 in) of 26-gauge (0.4 mm) sterling silver wire

Wire snippers

1 x 3 cm (1¼ in) silver coloured brooch back and sieve.

Snipe-nose pliers

Approx. 24 x 3 cm (1¼ in) dyed grey petal shaped mother-of-pearl side-drilled beads

1 x 5 cm (2 in) sterling silver headpin

Round-nose pliers

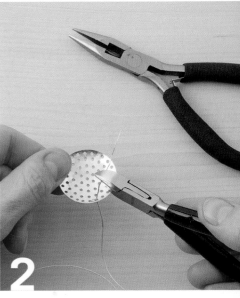

1 Snip a 60 cm (24 in) length of 26-gauge (0.4 mm) sterling silver wire. Insert 5 cm (2 in) at one end of the wire down through a hole in the outer ring of holes in the sieve. Bring the end to the right side through the next hole to the left. Repeat to secure the wire in place.

2 Use a pair of snipe-nose pliers to pull the wire 'stitches' tight. Snip off the excess wire under the sieve.

3 Thread a 3 cm (1¼ in) petal shaped mother-of-pearl dyed grey side-drilled bead onto the wire. Slip the bead down the wire. Insert the wire through the second hole to the left, positioning the bead over the anchored wire with the bead pointing outwards. Pull the wire tight.

4 Bring the wire to the right side, four holes to the right hand side. Thread on a petal bead. Insert the wire through the second hole to the left. Pull the wire tight.

5 Repeat Step 4 to fix beads all around the outer ring of holes, using a pair of snipe-nose pliers to pull the wire tight as you work. When you are close to running out of wire, sew the

end of the wire twice between two holes in the sieve. Snip off the excess wire under the sieve. Repeat Step 1 to continue with the next length of wire.

6 Bring the wire to the right side through a hole in the second ring of holes. Thread on a petal bead. Insert the wire through the second hole to the left. Pull the wire tight. Bring the wire to the right side, four holes to the right hand side. Repeat to fix petal beads all around the second ring of beads.

7 Bring the wire to the right side through a hole in the third ring of holes. Thread on a petal bead. Insert the wire through the second hole to the left. Pull the wire tight. Bring the

wire to the right side, four holes to the right hand side. Repeat to fix petal beads all around the third ring of beads.

8 Bring the wire to the right side through any empty hole. Insert the wire to the wrong side through the next hole. Repeat to secure the wire in place. Use a pair of snipe-nose pliers to pull the wire tight. Snip off the excess wire under the sieve.

9 Thread on an 8 mm (⁵⁄₁₆ in) round jet bead onto a 5 cm (2 in) sterling silver headpin. Insert the headpin down through the centre of the sieve.

VARIATION: This pretty ring has sapphire blue glass spear shaped beads fixed to a small sieve and ring back. An amethyst bead sits at the centre.

10 Snip the wire of the headpin 1 cm (⅜ in) below the sieve with a pair of wire snippers.

11 Bend the extending wire into a loop with a pair of round-nose pliers. Lay the loop flat against the underside of the sieve.

12 Place the sieve on the brooch back. Squeeze the prongs of the brooch back over the edge of the sieve with a pair of snipe-nose pliers.

Cluster stud earrings

Crystals and pearls in autumnal shades combine on this delightful pair of stud earrings. The tiny beads are fixed to ballpins and cluster on each earring around a large glass pearl threaded on an eye pin.

YOU WILL NEED

2 x 4 mm (⅛ in) light rose bicone crystal beads

2 x 4 mm (⅛ in) black diamond bicone crystal beads

6 light gold rondel freshwater pearl beads

24 x 3.5 cm (1⅜ in) gold-filled ballpins

Round-nose pliers

Snipe-nose pliers

Wire snippers

2 x 1.2 cm (½ in) diameter copper coloured glass pearl beads

2 x 5 cm (2 in) gold-filled eye pins

4 coral potato freshwater pearl beads

8 x 6 mm (¼ in) light colorado facetted rondel crystal beads

2 x 4 mm (⅛ in) rose bicone crystal beads

2 x 4 mm (⅛ in) topaz bicone crystal beads

Pair of gold-filled earring studs with rings

VARIATION: The soft green and white colour scheme give a Summery feel to this pair of charming earrings. Each earring has a 1.5 cm (⅝ in) diameter white glass pearl threaded on a sterling silver ballpin. Triangular peridot beads and opalite chips with wrapped loops are threaded on and topped with mother-of-pearl and opalite chips.

1 Slip a 4 mm (⅙ in) light rose bicone crystal bead, a 4 mm (⅙ in) black diamond bicone crystal bead and a light gold rondel freshwater pearl onto three 3.5 cm (1⅜ in) gold-filled ballpins. Refer to the **Making a wrapped loop technique** on page 19 to make a wrapped loop above each bead.

2 Open the eye of a 5 cm (2 in) gold-filled eye pin using two pairs of pliers. Slip the loops of the wrapped beads onto the eye. Close the eye with two pairs of pliers. Thread a 1.2 cm (½ in) diameter copper coloured glass pearl bead onto the eye pin.

3 Slip two coral potato freshwater pearl beads and three 6 mm (¼ in) light colorado facetted rondel crystal beads onto five 3.5 cm (1⅜ in) gold-filled ballpins. Refer to the **Making a wrapped loop technique** on page 19 to make a wrapped loop above each bead. Thread the wrapped beads onto the eye pin.

4 Slip a 4 mm (⅙ in) rose bicone crystal bead, a 4 mm (⅙ in) topaz bicone crystal bead and two light gold rondel freshwater pearls onto four 3.5 cm (1⅜ in) gold-filled ballpins. Refer to the **Making a single loop technique** on page 18 to make a single loop above each bead.

5 Thread the beads onto the eye pin. Holding the eye pin upright, splay the beads outwards from the eye pin. Thread a light colorado facetted rondel crystal bead onto the eye pin.

6 Refer to the **Making a wrapped loop technique** on page 19 to make a wrapped loop above the bead, wrapping the wire tightly around the eye pin to press the rondel crystal bead down onto the loops of wire.

7 Carefully open the ring on the earring stud with a pair of pliers. Slip the wrapped loop onto the ring. Close the ring using the pliers. Make a matching earring.

Hoop earrings

A pair of plain hoop earrings have been jazzed up with hanging apatite chips to create a fabulous gypsy style. The earrings are simple to make, with sterling silver discs hanging amongst the chips on ballpins.

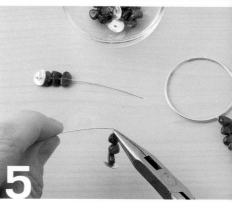

YOU WILL NEED

Masking tape

Round-nose pliers

10 x 8 mm (⁵⁄₁₆ in) sterling silver discs

50 apatite smooth chips

30 x 5 cm (2 in) sterling silver ballpins

Pair of sterling silver hoop earrings

Snipe-nose pliers

Wire snippers

VARIATION: The green aventure triangular beads look very elegant on this pair of gold-filled hoops. Two beads are threaded on the centre ballpin with four single beads suspended at each side.

1 Stick a strip of masking tape around one jaw of a pair of round-nose pliers 4 mm (⅙ in) from the tip. This will help to keep the loop you make on the ballpins that suspend the chips large enough to slip onto the earring hoops.

2 Thread an 8 mm (⁵⁄₁₆ in) sterling silver disc and five apatite smooth chips onto a 5 cm (2 in) sterling silver ballpin. If the smooth chips you have are graduated in size, use the largest for this ballpin as it will be at the centre of the hoop. Set aside five of the larger chips for the centre of the other earring.

3 Refer to the **Making a wrapped loop technique** on page 19 to make a wrapped loop

above the chips, placing the loop at the 4 mm (⅙ in) position on the round-nose pliers.

4 Slip the loop onto a hoop. Close the hoop and hold it at the top so the chips hang down from the centre. Gently squeeze the loop around the hoop with a pair of snipe-nose pliers to secure the ballpin in place.

5 Thread a sterling silver disc and three apatite smooth chips onto two ballpins. Make a wrapped loop above the chips as before. Thread the loops onto the hoop each side of the first loop. Gently squeeze the loops around the hoop with a pair of snipe-nose pliers to secure the ballpin in place as before, positioning the loops 3 mm (⅛ in) apart.

6 Thread a sterling silver disc and two apatite smooth chips onto two ballpins. Make a wrapped loop above the chips as before. Thread the loops onto the hoop each side of the three hanging loops. Gently squeeze the loops around the hoop with a pair of snipe-nose pliers to secure the ballpin in place as before.

7 Thread an apatite smooth chip onto ten ballpins. Make a wrapped loop above each chip as before. Thread five loops onto the hoop each side of the fixed hanging loops. Gently squeeze the loops around the hoop with a pair of snipe-nose pliers to secure the ballpin in place as before. Make a matching earring.

103

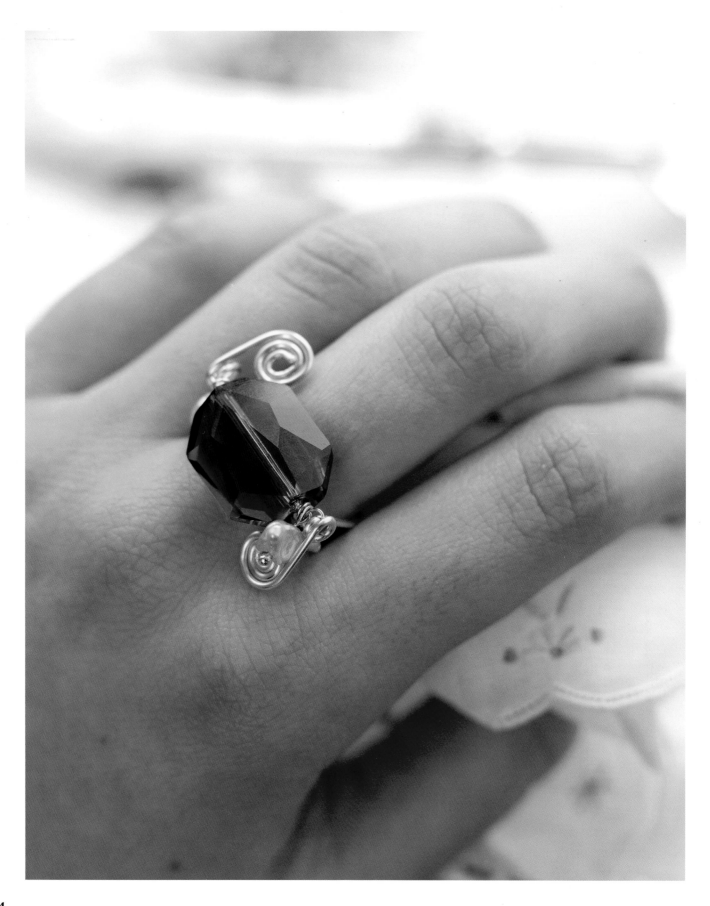

Spiral ring

This attention-seeking ring is created using a variety of techniques. The dramatic wire coils are simple to make. The wire is held with a pair of plastic-tipped pliers which will not mark the wire whilst you work.

YOU WILL NEED

Approx. 12 cm (4¾ in) of 26-gauge (0.4 mm) sterling silver wire

Snipe-nose pliers

Round-nose pliers

Wire snippers

1.8 x 1.5 cm (1¹⁄₁₆ x ⅝ in) amethyst facetted hexagonal crystal bead

16 cm (6¼ in) of 31-gauge (1 mm) sterling silver wire

Jewellery file

2 x 3 mm (⅛ in) sterling silver oval beads

2 white keshi pearl beads

4 x 3.5 cm (1⅜ in) sterling silver ballpins

Mandrel

Plastic-tipped pliers

1 Hold a length of 26-gauge (0.4 mm) sterling silver wire 4 cm (1½ in) from one end with a pair of snipe-nose pliers. Using your fingers, bend the wire over the jaws at a right angle.

2 Make a loop above the bend of the wire using a pair of round-nose pliers, ending up with the end of wire again at right angles to the main wire.

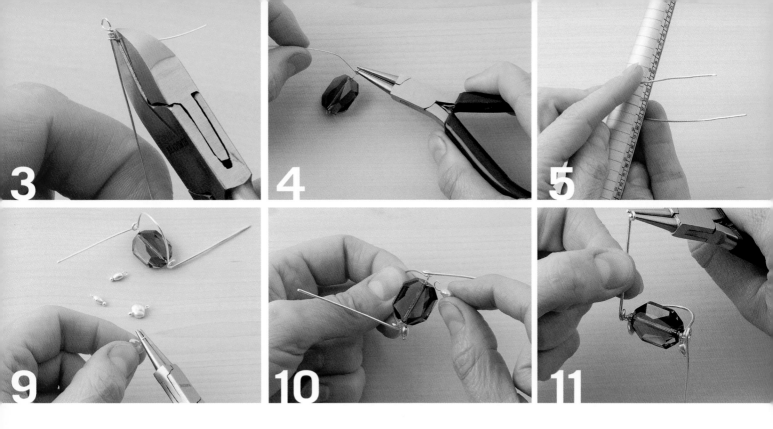

3 With the round-nose pliers slipped through the loop to hold the wire steady, wrap the end of the wire neatly around the main wire four times. Snip off the excess wire close to the wrapped wire. Squeeze the snipped end close to the wrapped wire with a pair of snipe-nose pliers.

4 Thread on a 1.8 x 1.5 cm (1 1/16 x 5/8 in) amethyst facetted hexagonal crystal bead. Refer to the **Making a wrapped loop technique** on page 19 to make a wrapped loop at the other end of the bead, making the loop 2 mm (1/12 in) above the bead.

5 File the ends of a 16 cm (6 1/4 in) length of 31-gauge (1 mm) sterling silver wire with a jewellery file to round the ends. Hold the ends of the wire and bend it around a mandrel 3 mm (1/8 in) above the size level required.

6 Thread the wrapped loops of the crystal bead onto the wire ends. Slip the bead down the wires to rest against the mandrel at the size level required. Hold the wire below one wrapped loop with a pair of snipe-nose pliers. Use your fingers to bend the wire downwards. Repeat to bend the wire above the bead upwards.

7 Slip the ring off the mandrel. Hold the wire behind the lower wrapped loop with the tips of a pair of round-nose pliers. Wrap the extending wire tightly around the tip until it is pointing upwards.

8 Adjust the jaws of the pliers and bend the wire downwards. Squeeze the coils of the wire together with a pair of snipe-nose pliers. Repeat at the other end of the wire.

9 Thread two 3 mm (1/8 in) sterling silver oval beads and two white keshi pearl beads onto four 3.5 cm (1 3/8 in) sterling silver ballpins. Refer to the **Making a single loop technique** on page 18 to make a single loop above the beads.

106

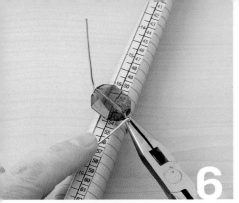
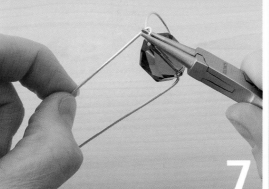
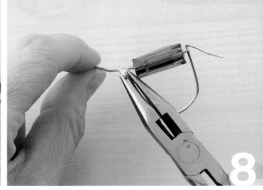
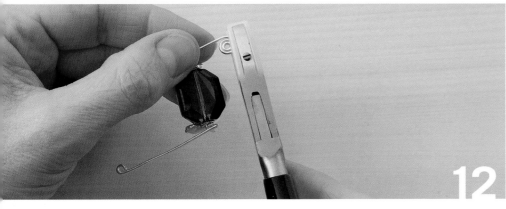

VARIATION: Give a ring a South Western style by using a turquoise bead as the feature bead with a pair of light gold freshwater pearls on ballpins at each side.

10 Open the loops of the silver and pearl beads. Slip a silver bead and pearl bead onto the wrapped wire at each side of the crystal bead. Close the single loops.

11 Hold the end of the lower wire between the tips of a pair of round-nose pliers. Bend the wire into a circle, facing inwards. Repeat on the upper wire.

12 Holding the circle tightly with a pair of plastic-tipped pliers, coil the wire tightly around one circle. Keep adjusting the grip of the pliers to bend the wire smoothly until you reach the edge of the crystal bead. Repeat on the upper wire.

Woven bead lariat

A bead loom is a practical device to create a long woven strip of beads. The long length of this sparkling lariat means that it can be worn in various ways and even as a belt. The ends are finished with contrast coloured stripes and a fringe incorporating bicone crystals. Size 9 rocaille beads are the most versatile size for weaving. It is economical to use quilting thread for this project as a large amount of thread is needed.

YOU WILL NEED

Quilting thread

Bead loom

Water or air erasable pen

Long beading needle

10 g (¼ oz) size 9 aquamarine glass rocaille beads

80 g (2¾ oz) size 9 silver lined clear glass rocaille beads

28 x 5 mm (¼ in) indicolite faceted round crystals

42 x 4 mm (⅛ in) jet AB bicone crystals

1 Cut fourteen 170 cm (68 in) lengths of quilting thread. These are the warp threads which will lay lengthwise in the loom. Tie the threads together with a knot at one end. Lay the threads level and mark them 25 cm (10 in) and 135 cm (54 in) from the knot with a water or air erasable pen. Allow the ink to dry. Divide the bundle in two and slip the knot under the nail head on one of the wooden rollers.

2 Hold the threads taut and turn the roller to wind the warp threads until the pen marks reach the grooves of the metal spring. Tighten the wing nut to hold the roller in place.

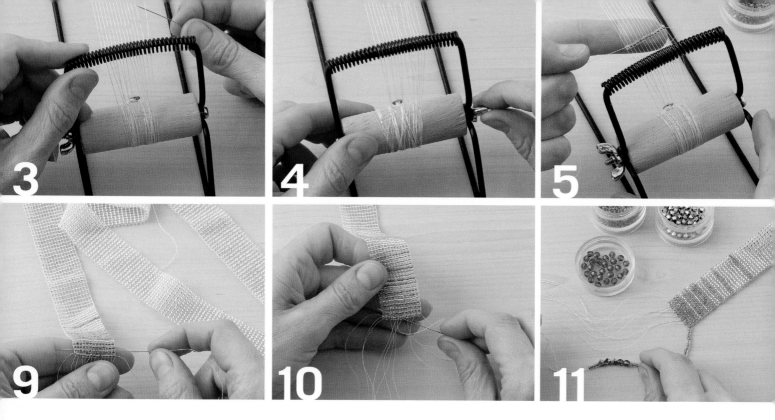

3 Position the threads in the grooves of the metal spring, separating the threads with a needle. Turn the loom so that the roller and the metal spring you have been working on is furthest from you. Position the threads in the grooves of the metal spring that is nearest to you, holding the threads taut.

4 Keeping the threads taut, knot the thread ends together. Slip the knot under the nail. Turn the roller to wind the threads around it. Tighten the wing nut to hold the threads taut.

5 Thread a long length of thread onto a long beading needle. This will be the weft thread. Tie the thread to an outside thread close to the pen marks on

the roller nearest you, leaving a 15 cm (6 in) trailing end of thread. Thread on thirteen size 9 aquamarine glass rocaille beads for the first row and slip them down the weft thread. Position the thread at right angles under the warp threads then press them up between the warp threads with a finger.

6 Insert the needle back through the beads, making sure that the needle passes above the warp threads to secure the beads in place.

7 Pick up the next row of aquamarine beads and repeat the process. Work a sequence of four rows of aquamarine beads, one row of silver beads, two rows of

aquamarine beads, one row of silver beads, two rows of aquamarine beads, two rows of silver beads, one row of aquamarine beads, three rows of silver beads, one row of aquamarine beads, six rows of silver beads, one row of aquamarine beads. Push the rows of beads together as you work to keep them neat.

8 Continue working rows of silver beads. When you run out of thread, weave the thread back through the rows of beads. Add a new thread as described in Step 5 and continue. When you reach the second roller, loosen the tension on the rollers and roll the beadwork onto the roller to continue until you reach the pen marks on the threads.

9 Weave one row of aquamarine beads, six rows of silver beads, one row of aquamarine beads, three rows of silver beads, one row of aquamarine beads, two rows of silver beads, two rows of aquamarine beads, one row of silver beads, two rows of aquamarine beads, one row of silver beads, four rows of aquamarine beads. Loosen the tension on the rollers and remove the work. Cut off the knots. Thread the trailing first weft thread onto a needle. Work the thread back into the work.

10 Starting with the second thread, weave every other thread at the ends of the lariat and the ends of newly joined threads back into the work, leaving seven extending threads for the fringe at each end of the lariat. Cut off the ends of the threads woven back into the beadwork.

11 Thread the first thread onto a needle. To make the fringe, thread on forty aquamarine beads, two 5 mm (¼ in) indicolite faceted round crystals, three 4 mm (⅙ in) jet AB bicone crystals and four aquamarine rocaille beads.

12 Insert the needle back through all the beads except the last three rocaille beads, work the thread through the beadwork. Make a fringe of seven hanging beads at each end of the lariat. Cut off the ends of the threads after weaving them back into the beadwork.

VARIATION: This 70 cm (27½ in) long lariat is woven with eight threads using blue rocaille beads and sapphire bicone crystals.

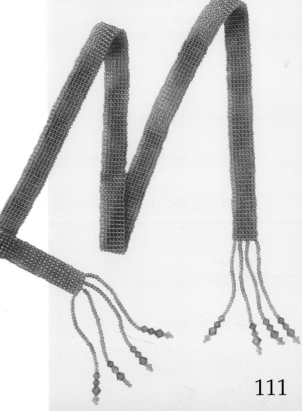

INDEX